AN
ORDINARY WOMAN
IN
EXTRAORDINARY TIMES

IBOLYA (SZALAI) GROSSMAN

To
Sandor Eisen
with my best
wishes!

Ili Grossman

Nov/00

Nemelem tetszeni
fog a könyvem.
Ili

Introduction Gabriele Scardellato

The Multicultural History Society of Ontario
1990

AN
ORDINARY WOMAN
IN
EXTRAORDINARY TIMES

IBOLYA (SZALAI) GROSSMAN

This is a volume in the MHSO series *Ethnocultural Voices*.

The Multicultural History Society of Ontario is a resource centre on the campus of the University of Toronto. It was created in 1976 by a group of academics, civil servants, librarians and archivists who saw a need for a special effort to preserve materials relevant to the province's immigrant and ethnic history. The Society receives support from the Ministry of Culture and Communications of the Province of Ontario, the Honourable Hugh O'Neil, Minister.

Canadian Cataloguing in Publication Data

Grossman, Ibolya (Szalai), b. 1916
AN ORDINARY WOMAN IN EXTRAORDINARY TIMES

(Ethnocultural voices)
ISBN 0-919045-46-4

1. Grossman, Ibolya Szalai, 1916-   .   2. Refugees,
Jewish — Canada — Biography.   3. Hungarians —
Canada — Biography.   4. Immigrants — Canada —
Biography.   5. Hungary — Politics and government —
1945-   .   6. Hungary — Politics and government —
1918-1945.   7.Hungary — Social conditions.
I. Multicultural History Society of Ontario
II. Title.   III. Series.

FC106.H95G76 1990   971'.00494511   C90-095286-5
F1035.H8G76 1990

Published 1990

Printed and bound in Canada 〈≣〉13

Contents

Dedication

To the memory of my parents Szalai Ignacz and Laura, who were killed by the Nazis in 1944.

* * *

I wrote my life story at the request of my son, Andy and I dedicate it to him, his wife, Magdi, and my two beloved grandchildren, David and Kati.

* * *

I would like to express my gratitude to my creative writing teachers, Barbara Turner, Maria Gould and Jayne Brinklow who helped and encouraged me to write stories about my past which I later collected to form this autobiography. As a person writing in my second language I often doubted if I could write my story. On one occasion Jayne Brinklow wrote the following on one of my efforts; "Do not be discouraged by the red marks! This is the icing only .... You have baked a lovely cake!"

Preface

The experiences of immigrants and members of ethnic groups are raw material for historians, but they are also much more. Told in the voices of the individuals themselves, in memoirs, diaries, autobiographies and reminiscences, they have an immediacy that no third-person account can match. They kindle our imaginations and touch our hearts. For this reason the series Ethnocultural Voices while it contributes to scholarly study of ethnocultural history also increases public awareness and understanding of the diverse origins and experiences of Ontario's peoples.

Ibolya Grossman's story is that of a Hungarian-Jewish woman who in her early adult years experienced World War II and some time later the October Revolution. In Canada, she supported her son and herself by a variety of jobs first in Winnipeg and then in Toronto. The adjective she applied to herself in the title of her reminiscence will not be accepted as appropriate by her readers. The indomitable spirit with which she confronted her times is far from ordinary. So also is the mastery she achieved of the English language, which she began to learn at the age of forty and employed to set down her story.

The Multicultural History Society of Ontario is proud to publish Ibi Grossman's reminiscence, and is grateful to its Resource Centre Coordinator, Dr. Gabriele Scardellato, for his introduction and able editing of her manuscript.

Jean Burnet
Multicultural History Society of Ontario
1990

Introduction

Mrs. Grossman's autobiography forms part of the history of Hungarian migration and immigration to Canada, a topic which has been better served by historians than have the histories of many other immigrant groups.* The beginning of a significant migration to Canada from Hungary dates from the end of the nineteenth century and the subsequent movement of both sojourners and settlers to this country has occurred in three, or possibly four main phases. The first phase, described as the "Saskatchewan period," embraces migration to Canada up to the First World War. The second phase covers the inter-war years, but more specifically the 1920s, and the third phase encompasses the immigration which occurred immediately after the Second World War by people who were displaced by it. The fourth phase, lasting barely eighteen months, applies to the immigration of Hungarians fleeing the aftermath of the suppressed Revolution of 1956 and is the one for which Mrs. Grossman's experiences are most relevant. Mass migration from Hungary to the New World began in the 1880s and was primarily a rural phenomenon, a consequence of overpopulation and poverty in the Hungarian countryside. This migration, from what was then the Kingdom of Hungary, was an ethnically diverse movement which included not only Hungarians but also Jews, Germans, Croatians, Ruthenians, Romanians, and so forth. Estimates of the total number of emigrants from Hungary who reached North America before the outbreak of the First World War vary between 640,000 and 1,000,000. Regardless of which figure is held to be the most accurate, a very small portion of this number reached Canada. Again, there is some uncertainty about this total, which has been cited as anything from 8,000 to 15,000.

The major settlements of Hungarians in Canada which were created through this phase of Hungarian immigration were located on the Canadian prairies, in particular in the territory which would become the province of Saskatchewan. This movement to the prairies occurred initially as part of a migration strategy which led Hungarians first to the industrial labour markets of the United States of America. From there they found their way to western Canada and Saskatchewan and Manitoba in particular. Thus, by 1914 Hungarian Canadians were to be found primarily in farming communities on the prairies. Smaller groups became established in urban settings in other parts of Canada including, in Ontario, Welland, Hamilton, Niagara Falls, Windsor, and Brantford. These latter groupings would prove to be very important for the next major phase of Hungarian immigration to Canada.

Some 33,000 Hungarians emigrated to Canada in the interwar years. Unusually, this figure was exceeded only slightly by the number of Hungarians, some 38,500, who entered the United States over the same period. Of course, the two figures are intimately connected in that the restrictionist immigration policy adopted by the United States in 1924 helped to increase the number of Hungarians who chose Canada as their target for immigration. Equally important, it was through this phase of Hungarian immigration to Canada that the nature of Hungarian Canadian settlement in this country was changed drastically.

Though they arrived generally as agricultural labourers, thereby attempting to benefit from the Canadian version of American restrictionism, they were a more diversified group occupationally than their pre-First World War predecessors and their numbers included a substantial portion of skilled artisans. It is ironic, given that Hungarian immigration in this period was intended to reinforce the country's agricultural labour force, that instead it coincided with, and contributed significantly to, the redistribution of Hungarian Canadians from predominantly rural settings to urban ones. A number of new settlements were created in Canadian cities through this period and those which already existed increased in size. The third phase of Hungarian immigration to Canada occurred in the aftermath of the Second World War and again differed significantly from those which had gone before.

In general, Canada benefitted enormously from the mass migration of people displaced by the war. In the five year period 1946 - 51, for example, almost 500,000 immigrants entered the country. Over five thousand of these were Hungarians and more than half of them settled in Ontario. This influx peaked in the following year with the arrival of a further 4500 immigrants. Through this immigration Toronto's Hungarian settlement experienced the largest growth of any Canadian city with an additional 1,100 Hungarian immigrants having settled in the city by 1951. Second was Montreal with some 800 Hungarians followed by Hamilton, Ontario, with roughly 250. Apart from these central Canadian cities, Winnipeg was the only urban centre which attracted more than 200 Hungarian immigrants.

The fourth major phase of Hungarian immigration to Canada, and the one which is most relevant for the autobiography reproduced below, occurred still within the era of post-World War Two migration but it derived its impetus from renewed turmoil in the sending country. The Hungarian Revolution of 1956 has been dubbed "the most important event in the history of Canada's Hungarian community." (Driesziger, 1982, 203) It was important because it resulted in the arrival of some 38,000 refugees in Canada and because of the attention which it focussed within the country on events in Hungary.

In Ontario, demonstrations in support of the Revolution were held in a number of cities, including Ottawa and Toronto, as well as a number of smaller centres. A national relief programme was created and this effort eventually collected close to $900,000. When the Revolution was suppressed in November of 1956 the Canadian public appears to have been well-disposed to assist with the accommodation of some of the 200,000 or so refugees who fled their native land. This favourable disposition was enhanced by an expanding Canadian economy and thus, an equally well-disposed federal government. In sharp contrast to more recent events in Ontario and elsewhere across the country, the decision of the town council of a small community in northern Ontario not to accept any Hungarians because "they don't screen them enough" and "they will just make trouble here," was received with "public outrage so great that within twenty-four hours the town council withdrew the statement and offered the refugees assistance." (Papp, *Polyphony*, 1979-80, 66)

As readers of Mrs. Grossman's autobiography will note, she, and probably many other refugees who fled Hungary in the aftermath of November 1956, were totally unaware of conditions — social, economic or political — which awaited them in Canada. Indeed, many of them may well have chosen Canada because, as Mrs. Grossman says, the Canadian embassy in Vienna was open while that of the United States was not. In this, as in many other details, Mrs. Grossman's reminiscences should prove instructive for those interested in Canada's immigration history. There is in her account, for example, far less about typical "push and pull" factors in migration than one might expect. As a reader I was not struck by a particular political urgency in Mrs. Grossman's desire to leave her native land or by any particular and overwhelming economic motivation, two of the classic "push" factors. Moreover, there is no hint of a "pull" factor in the sense of particular knowledge of better lifestyles elsewhere; for example, those possibly being lived by relatives who might serve as part of a network for emigration. Rather, the reality of immigration as suggested by Mrs. Grossman is much more richly textured and complex in its motivation than we might conclude if we were to label her simply a refugee of the events of 1956 in Hungary.

To begin with, her immigration must include as central her identity as a Jewish Hungarian and the persecution which she endured in her native land because of it. The experiences to which she and her relatives were subjected at the hands of her fellow Hungarians, to say nothing of the atrocities which resulted in the deaths of relatives and loved ones, were clearly powerful components in her decision to leave Hungary. With this we must also combine more common factors like the severely crowded living conditions which she was forced to endure in the post-war period. The discomfort of those conditions must have been exacerbated by the knowledge that any protest, regardless of how carefully worded or how amply justified in reality, would produce even greater distress in loved ones already suffering from the catastrophe of the recent past.

Finally, we cannot ignore the fact of gender and of Mrs. Grossman's personal status at the time of immigration. She carried, and did so with remarkable strength, the dual burden of her widowhood and her responsibility for her son. Of course, the presence of parents in various immigrations, Hungarian or other, is not unusual. The presence of single females to say nothing of mothers and especially single mothers travelling with their children is far less usual. In the literature of migration it is not difficult to find examples of widowers who migrate and leave children behind, usually in the company of family, in order to make better provision for them. Women have adopted similar migration strategies, notably those who come as domestics. But it is much rarer to find single parents of either gender undertaking migration or immigration with their children by their side. Clearly, Mrs. Grossman's decision to find a better future for her son and herself deserves to be noted for the wonderful courage which it required. As Jean Burnet states in her *Preface*, her autobiography indeed serves to "kindle our imaginations and touch our hearts."

Gabriele Scardellato
Multicultural History Society of Ontario
1990

---

* The brief sketch of Hungarian Canadian migration and immigration history presented here owes much to the efforts of a number of fine scholars to whom I am greatly indebted. The main works consulted are listed below and readers wishing to be better informed would do well to begin with these titles. Special thanks is owed to Dr. N.F. Driesziger who applied his expertise in reading Mrs. Grossman's manuscript before publication.

Driesziger, N. F., M.L. Kovacs, Paul Bödy and Bennett Kovrig, *Struggle and Hope: The Hungarian-Canadian Experience*, McClelland & Stewart with Supply & Services Canada: Toronto, 1982.

Patrias, Carmela, *The Kanadai Magyar Ujsag and the Politics of the Hungarian Canadian Elite*, The Multicultural History Society of Ontario: Toronto, 1978

"Hungarians in Ontario," *Polyphony: The Bulletin of the Multicultural History Society of Ontario*, vol. 2, no. 2-3, 1979-80. This special issue of the Society's Bulletin is devoted exclusively to the subject of Hungarians in Ontario and includes the work of a number of scholars of Hungarian Canadian immigration including the issue editor Susan M. Papp, Carmela Patrias, Nandor F. Driesziger, and George Bisztray. Their contributions to this issue of the Bulletin have proven to be extremely useful.

Prologue

My dictionary

For some strange reason, I still use my old tattered Hungarian-English dictionary which I bought in Winnipeg in the summer of 1957. I remember that summer day very well. I got off the bus at the wrong stop and consequently I had a long walk to the bookstore in a temperature of one hundred and one degrees fahrenheit.

On the first page of the book now I see my son's signature, "Reti Andras," his name in Hungarian twice underlined to be sure that the dictionary is his. Under his name is mine "Reti Ibolya" the family name of my first late husband, and our first address, 130 Mackray St., Winnipeg. Under it another two addresses in Winnipeg and my son's name again, this time in English "Andrew Reti" and the address 301/A Markham St., Toronto. There are another four addresses including that of our present home.

The dictionary's pages are all loose, every one of them, and so are the brown front and back covers. Most of the pages are torn and some are hardly legible. As I carefully turn the pages I find an old yellow piece of paper cut out of a Hungarian newspaper in 1963. It says that we welcome my in-laws Reti Henrik and his wife, Janka, from Hungary and that they are the first couple allowed to visit Canada. It also says that they will celebrate their fiftieth wedding anniversary with us here in Toronto.

Why do I still treasure this piece of paper? And why do I still use this dictionary instead of a new and better one? They are mementos. One of the first things in my new life. The book became a symbol of freedom to me when I bought it on that hot summer day many years ago. This dictionary has helped me to speak English. This dictionary has helped me to write. And I have many things in my mind to write about. As I put them down on paper, I still use my faithful dictionary.

* * *

My childhood

Sunday mornings when our mother got up but father was still in bed, my younger sister Elizabeth and I jumped into mother's bed and begged our father "Please, father, tell us more stories about your past." And father told us — two little girls of four and five — stories that I liked very much to hear. Father was a slightly built man with dark, almost black hair and blue eyes. This contrast made him very handsome; an impression increased by his perky mustache. He was blessed with an optimistic personality. In addition to his good humour he was always ready to help those in need.

I try to recollect some of his stories. One of my favourites is funny. As a young man my father wandered from village to village looking for a job. It was in the late eighteen hundreds or in 1890 and because he was born in 1872 he must have been about eighteen years old. One time, when father had no money left, he knocked on a door in a small village and asked for food. Probably he didn't look like a beggar, because the little girl who opened the door for him ran to the inner room shouting; "Mother, come quickly, there is a gentleman beggar in the doorway."

Another of his stories was so sad that as a little girl I cried when I heard it. It happened during One when the two sides were in hand-to-hand combat. Father faced a Russian soldier. Both had bayonets in their hands. My father was a split second faster and stabbed his enemy. But when the Russian soldier fell back with a scream, "Shma Jiszroel," which is Hebrew for "Hear, oh my God," father was shocked.

With tears in his eyes he whispered, "I killed a Jew." But it was war and he would have been killed if the other soldier had been faster.

When father got older he stopped wandering, settled down and got married. Unfortunately, his wife died after a few years of marriage and he was left with two little girls on his hands. The girls were four and eight years of age. The only solution was for him to get married again. But with two small girls it was very difficult. Soon after his wife's death he was introduced to a girl. She was in her early thirties and was willing to marry him and be a stepmother to the girls. They moved to a bigger city where he opened a tinsmith shop. They also bought a small family home. Soon after their marriage in 1911, my sister, Aranka, was born in 1912. There were two more babies after Aranka, a boy and a girl who both died in infancy; then I was born and a year after me my sister, Elizabeth.

We were born in Pécs, the capital of the Hungarian province of Baranya. I remember when I was still very young that mother cried very often. I didn't know why. It was much later that I learned the reason for her crying.

When I was four and my younger sister Elizabeth was three we started kindergarten. The kindergarten was close to our home so after a little while we went by ourselves, holding each other by the hand. I still have some vivid memories of my kindergarten years. We were occupied with many things like colouring papers, braiding little baskets, threading pearls for necklaces and playing games.

When the weather permitted we went to the yard to play. Sometimes two big boys, they must have been eight years old, came into the yard also. They were sons of one of the teachers. They always were after us small kids. With a thick rubber band in their hands they tried to pinch us. I was very afraid of them and tried to hide. But one boy caught me and pinched my arm. "It hurts!" I cried out loudly, holding back my tears.

There were some baby chickens in the yard, yellow, fluffy little things. We were told not to touch them. I would watch them as they ran after their mother and from time to time bent their heads to peck at the ground. How I wished to pick up one of them and pet its tiny body! One day a terrible thing happened. A boy stepped on one of the chicks. The baby chick died. The boy cried loudly, saying over and over that it was an accident, he hadn't meant to do it. For punishment he was separated from his classmates for the rest of the afternoon and was not allowed to play.

At lunch time we all went from the yard to the only school

room, which was huge. There was one long low table where we worked and drew. Along the wall were low benches where we sat to eat our lunch. All had to bring their own lunches. They brought the food in little baskets. The baskets were in different shapes and colours. The teacher would lift them up one by one asking, "Whose is this?" When we recognized our own, we went to get it and then went back to the bench where we were allowed to eat. After lunch we had to line up at the sink to have a drink of water from the same enamel cup. Then we went to the washroom in groups and after that back to the benches to have our nap. We sat down and had to put our head on the other child's shoulder. We either had to go to sleep or be quiet and motionless for a period of time. My neck hurt when we were allowed to stand up but I was afraid to complain.

After our nap some of the children got a slice of black bread. I always wanted a slice too. At home we didn't have black bread because mother baked two very big round white loaves every week, which tasted very good but weren't black. So one day I lined up for the bread with the others. As I took the first bite I looked up and saw my mother coming toward me. She shook her head in disapproval, took the bread out of my hand and gave it to the child nearest to me. I learned much later that despite our poverty mother was too proud to receive any charity. Even though we were poor our parents always provided food for the family.

Mother had a very difficult time with her two stepdaughters. Before their father's remarriage everybody had told them that a stepmother could be only bad and evil. Mother did everything she could to show them that she was not but nothing helped. The younger girl was very much under the influence of the older one.

I was four years old when I overhead my big sister Margaret saying, "Hurry into our room before our ice cream melts and we can eat it in peace."

I ran to my mother asking, "Mother, what is ice cream and why didn't you give me any?" Mother was surprised that they hadn't given the little ones any ice cream because she had told them to do so. I wished that my big sisters would give me just a little bite to taste. Because of them we smaller girls were deprived of many things.

Mother tried to please them and to show the girls that she wasn't a bad stepmother to them. We had a piano my parents had bought for the two oldest girls. In fact, they had borrowed money and had gone into debt in buying it. The girls took piano lessons. I remember that sometimes they had no money to pay the piano teacher so mother gave her some merchandise from our store instead. I loved to listen to that piano music so much! I always asked either Margaret or my other stepsister, Ilona, to play for us when we were put to bed.

It is from this period that I recall some early childhood fears of going to sleep. Many times in my half-sleep, when I took a step into the room, there was a gaping hole. If I tried to take a step in another direction again a hole blocked my way. As I looked around me the entire floor was full of holes. I wasn't fully asleep yet but I couldn't control my imagination. Finally I must have fallen asleep before I had time to cry out.

We had a black and white cat in our house. I remember that she didn't like any noise. When the girls washed dishes they dropped the cutlery noisily into the drawer. The cat gave a loud and indignant "meow" every time a fork, knife or spoon was dropped. The cat's favourite spot was a top shelf in the kitchen. When she heard the key in the keyhole at the entrance door she jumped down and ran to greet whoever in the family had come home. She was very faithful to the family. Once, when she had had a litter, mother sent her with one of the kittens to my auntie in another small city. I don't know how she managed it but some time later the cat showed up again at our door. She had come back from many, many kilometres away.

Our family home contained one bedroom for my parents, one room for the three smaller girls and a third room for Margaret and Ilona. Their room opened onto the yard. We also had a small dining room and a kitchen. We didn't have an indoor toilet or bathroom. The toilet was in the yard in a wooden booth. In the kitchen we had a sitting tub for bathing. We also had two sheds in the yard. In one, mother kept big quantities of flour, goose-fat, jam, sugar and other groceries needed in the household. The other shed was for wood for the stoves. To start a fire in the wood stove we first had to cut some wood very thin. Then mother put it into the stove through a small door, put some paper on top and lit it. When the flames were big enough mother added some thicker wood. Once I wanted to help to cut thin wood with a hatchet. Mother warned me not to do it but I did it anyway when she was not home. I almost cut off the index finger of my left hand when the hatchet came down as I was holding the piece of wood. I still bear the scar reminding me of my childhood misbehaviour.

The monthly wash was a big event. Mother hired a washerwoman and in a big wooden tub she washed the laundry all day long. It was the bedding which mother changed every month. I was so sorry for the woman when I saw her hands all wrinkled and white from the strong alkaline soap she used. On wash day, when I went to bed at night, I liked the smell of the freshly changed linen very much. Mother had light blue and pink checkered bedding with needlework around the edges of the pillows.

I remember a day when mother was sitting on a low chair in the kitchen. The chair was either Elizabeth's or mine. It had a brown wooden back and the seat was woven from strong, yellowish straw. Mother like to sit on the low, child-size chair. She was peeling potatoes and I saw that tears were pouring down her face. As a five-year-old I was scared that something terrible had happened. Mother always seemed a little unhappy and often wiped her tears but I had never thought much about it until this moment. "Why do you cry, mommy? Don't cry!" I said, putting my arms around her neck.

Mother wiped her tears and said, "Go put your good dress on, all of you are going to the synagogue."

"Is today a holiday?" I asked.

"No, today is no holiday but your big sister is going to get married," replied my mother.

"What is married?" I asked again.

"She will have a husband to live with, like your father and me." I ran to get dressed, still not knowing what all the crying and fuss was about. I felt very important when I saw the crowd in front of our house waiting for the bride to appear. Then a carriage with two horses came up to our door.

My younger big sister called out, "Margaret, the carriage is here!"

"Yes Ilona, I'm coming." Margaret came out from her room. I had never seen her so beautiful! She wore a white dress, a flower headress and lace around her forehead. A white veil hung down to her ankles. She went to the carriage with father and Ilona. There was a man in the carriage I had never seen before. Another man who was sitting at the front of the carriage touched the horses with his whip and they started to gallop. We, the smaller girls, did not ride with them. I was heartbroken.

Of course, I didn't know at that time that the situation between my mother and the two step-daughters was so bad that my oldest sister married the first man who asked her. My father was a good and soft-hearted man who couldn't do justice to his wife and daughters.

Ilona was at home a few more years after her sister's marriage but without Margaret's influence the situation became much better. Then Ilona got married also and it was a marriage of love.

Although my parents were not very religious, between them mother was the one who kept the Jewish traditions and cooked kosher meals. Friday night, which is the coming of the Sabbath, was my favourite of the entire week. The girls took turns cleaning the kitchen Friday afternoon for the Sabbath. I scrubbed the wooden floor and the black iron stove until they gleamed. I covered the table with white linen and put the copper candlesticks, which I also had to polish on it. Before sundown mother lit the candles. The sisters, Aranka, Elizabeth and I, circled around her waiting our turn to be blessed. "May the Almighty bless you, dear daughters, as he blessed our ancestors, Sarah, Rebecca, and Rachel."

Because of the hard times after the first World War my

parents didn't have many pleasures in their life. One of my father's few entertainments was his pipe which I very seldom saw him without. He also lit a cigar once a week. On his birthday or other exceptional occasions we always gave him a few good cigars as a present and he saved them for Sundays. Also, on Sunday afternoon, as his special treat, he went to the city's coffee house for his afternoon card game. Elizabeth and I used to visit him there, hoping that he was winning because then he would give us some money to buy candies or chocolate. But if he was losing the game he angrily sent us home.

Sometimes mother begged him not to go to the coffee house but to take the family for a picnic instead. We had a favourite place for these outings. It was a big park on a hill, called Tettye, which is a Turkish name. Many centuries ago Hungary was under Turkish occupation. Some ruins of a huge castle that had stood on that hill still remained. This was our favourite playground for hide and seek.

We girls loved to go on those infrequent outings. That was the only time our parents were really with us and paid attention to us. Any other time they were very busy with their daily routine and work. For our outing mother packed sandwiches and she bought soft drinks in little bottles from the vendors. Those drinks were sweet and red in colour. We also saw another vendor selling big, salty pretzels which he carried on a long stick held upright. We nagged our mother until she gave in and bought a pretzel for each of us. We spent a lovely afternoon in that park. My parents usually found some people to talk to, and my sisters and I played with their children.

Elementary school

I wasn't quite six years old when mother enrolled me in school. I went to a Jewish school for my first four years of education. While we always had food on the table, we could not have proper clothes. So from almost the very first day in school my classmates mocked me. Not that I was crippled or ugly; on the contrary, I was a pretty, petite child with huge brown eyes and black hair. However, I wasn't dressed like the other children. They noticed that I didn't have any underwear and that I wore a summer dress as a slip under my school dress during the winter. I also had a scarf which mother had made for me from a terry-cloth towel with a flower printed on it. I thought it was beautiful. I didn't know any better. Mother must have saved that towel because I had never seen it in use so I didn't even know what it might have been. We used only plain cotton towels. My classmates also mocked my cap which mother had made from a brown cotton stocking. She had cut off the upper part, sewed it together at one end and put a pom-pom on it. I was proud of my new cap. Without knowing it even the teacher hurt me. One day we learned about wool. The teacher, to demonstrate what it was, went to the rack where all the little coats were hanging and pointed to the ones made of wool. She didn't point to mine.

Once or twice a year, the children who were well off brought in some used clothing and the teacher gave it away to the less fortunate ones. My teacher, noticing how poorly I was dressed, offered some to me, but mother wouldn't let me accept anything. That attitude accompanied me through those first four years. Another time, in the third grade, I left my knitting at home when it was the day for handicraft class. I had to kneel on corn seed in the corner for the entire hour. I was terribly humiliated when the hour was finished and the entire class laughed at me as I returned to my seat.

I remember another very unpleasant episode. Most of the girls in the class were rich and spoiled. One day a girl named Edith approached me and asked, "Would you like to be my servant?" I wasn't quite sure what the word servant meant.

"What do I have to do as a servant?" I asked her.

"Not much," replied Edith. "You have to bring my coat from the rack, help me put it on, carry my schoolbag and all those things that a servant has to do. I will give you a pencil, a pen, or an eraser — maybe even some money."

"No, I don't want to be your servant!"

"As you wish," Edith said shrugging her shoulder. "I will find somebody else who will do it happily for me." Thinking of the things I might get from her, I reconsidered and accepted the offer.

The splinter

On the first Monday of every month my parents went to a market to sell goods from our store. In the tinsmith shop they owned father made cans, buckets, cake pans and other household items. We also had enamel pots and pans to sell. Mother was very busy helping sell the merchandise and also doing the house chores.

On one occasion, when I was about seven or eight years old, I was allowed to go to the market with my parents. They rented a huge carriage with two big strong horses to carry all the goods, which were carefully wrapped in straw. The market was an interesting place and as a child I liked to wander around. There were some tents but almost everything was just laid on the open ground or on long tables. First I had to help my parents unpack and carry the wares to the square which was appointed for their use. Merchandise was grouped together in the market. All textiles were in one row, porcelain and glass were in another, fresh food from the farms — dairy products, vegetables, fruits — again in other groups. I can still taste the freshly made butter which was sold on big green leaves by the peasant women.

There were tents where gingerbread was sold. They made so many things from it: animals, dolls small and big. But I liked the gingerbread hearts the best. They were beautifully decorated with colourful flowers made from sugar. On the brown gingerbread hearts, the pink, blue, yellow or red flowers were gorgeous and each had a small mirror in the centre of the heart. There were even some with inscriptions on them, like "My heart is yours forever" or "I give my heart to my sweetheart." I remember that once my mother bought me a small heart. I kept it for a while but it was so tempting that eventually I ate it.

My favourite part of the market was the toy section. I loved to look at the dolls, cradles, doll-carriages and doll houses. "Don't touch it!" a fat lady screamed at me when I tried to pet a doll's tiny hand. I jerked my hand back and just looked at the beauty. Her face was of rosy porcelain, she had big blue eyes with dark lashes and those eyes would open and close. She wore a pink silk dress, white socks, black patent shoes. She had a white pearl around her neck and a pink bow in her curly blonde hair. I looked at the other dolls also but went back to my favourite whom I called Piri. How I wished that Piri would be mine! To hold her, rock her, put her in my bed beside me at night and hug her close to me. I went back to tell mother about the precious doll.

As I started to say, "Mommy, I saw the most beautiful doll in the ..." my mother stopped me.

"You know that I don't have money for a doll or any other toys" she said. I knew that. All I wanted was to talk to her, to tell mother how nice Piri was. I had a rag doll only, which my sister Aranka made for each of us two smallest girls, but I never, never had another doll. The doll Aranka made was filled with sawdust which had started to come out from some parts of the doll's arms already. My heart was aching. I climbed up into the carriage and started to sweep the straw with my bare feet. Mother noticed and cried out, "Don't do it because a splinter will go into your sole." But in my anger and hurt I just continued until it really happened. A huge piece of wood went deep into my flesh. I was afraid to tell my mother because she had warned me earlier. Later I got hungry and climbed down to eat. Mother gave me a big white bun and sour cream for lunch. The rest of the afternoon I was very quiet because my leg hurt.

A few days later our next door neighbour looked at my leg and screamed to my mother, "Look at the child's leg! What happened to her? It is all swollen up." Only then did my mother take a closer look at my leg which was swollen from ankle to knee. I was scared when I saw adults so concerned about me. In answer to my mother's questions I told her about the accident in the market.

"Go wash your feet, we are going to Dr. Szanto," said mother.

"Do we take the streetcar, mother?" When she said yes I was happy because going on a streetcar was such a treat. After the doctor examined my foot he asked me if I was a brave girl. "Yes," I said but I shivered with fright when I saw the instruments the doctor took out. He didn't have an assistant so he called his own mother from the other room to hold my leg. I closed my eyes tightly to be ready for pain. But it wasn't so bad and after the doctor finished and bandaged by foot he gave me a couple of candies for my bravery. I was glad it was over because that meant another ride on the streetcar.

Because Elizabeth and I were close in age we played together a lot as small girls. We played house with our rag doll and our tiny naked porcelain doll which was only about three inches tall. The dolls could move their arms but not their legs. I didn't have that small doll long anyway because being porcelain it broke into pieces when I accidently dropped it.

When we played we spread our few toys on the kitchen table and kneeled on chairs to help us reach them. We took our dolls to visit each other, put them on the furniture we made from boxes and covered with little coloured rags. I even made a doll carriage from a shoe box. At one end I put the lid of the box upright. On the opposite end I fastened string to allow me to pull my carriage. For the inside I made curtains from two panels of cloth and also a blanket and pillow. We were so involved in our play we spoke to our dolls as if they were real babies.

On the rare occasion when we got some sweets, I pretended that I had already finished mine but I hid the last piece behind my back and said to Elizabeth "I finished my chocolate. If you give me yours you are an angel, if not, then you are a devil." Elizabeth would give it to me and afterwards I would show her mine in my hand to tease her. We fought as most sisters do and one time when we wanted to make it up an accident happened. Elizabeth was standing on a chair beside the lit stove. On the stove there was a pot with milk put to boil. As she bent down to kiss me she tipped the pot and the boiling milk poured on my thigh. I cried with the pain. The cold water I poured on it immediately made a huge blister.

Our sister, Aranka, was't very happy about having us around because she was five and six years older and she often had to baby-sit. I was the middle child and I was often left out. Elizabeth was a sickly baby from birth and needed more attention and special food. Aranka was older so she came first when a winter coat or a pair of shoes was needed. But I was always on good terms with my older sister and when we were fighting I was always the one who apologized, no matter whose fault it was.

I don't remember either pair of grandparents but I think that on my father's side they had passed away long ago. I remember my mother's mother whom I saw only once and who didn't speak Hungarian well. She lived in another town with her unmarried daughter, Hermina. I must have been only six years old when mother pressed me to write a letter to grandma. Because I had heard mother say so many times, "My hands are shaking," I started my letter, "Dear grandma; Forgive me my ugly writing but my hands are shaking."

Mother had two sisters whom I knew. One was Auntie Cili who lived in Budapest, our capital city, with her two grown daughters. The other sister, Matilda, lived in a smaller city, Ozora. One year mother took me to visit Auntie Cili. Some of the events of this visit I still remember.

My mother and I travelled by train from Pécs to Budapest, a trip of six hours. After we got off the train, we had a short distance to walk to Auntie Cili's apartment. We had to pass a big amusement park on our way. "Mother, Look!" I pulled her by the hand to a merry-go-round. "Look! Those big horses and deer and those carriages! How fast they are going round!"

"Would you like to have a ride?" she asked.

"Yes! Yes! I would!" We waited until it stopped and I chose a big carriage and sat down. Another little girl climbed into it and took the seat across from me. It was such a beautiful creation, that carriage. The seats were made of red velvet with two huge angels on either side, their hands spread out above our heads like they were protecting us from something bad. Then the whole thing started to go slowly round in circles. "Hi, mother!" I waved to her. But it went faster by the second and I couldn't see her any more. My eyes were tightly shut and I was holding onto the bar with both hands. Already I wished to stop it. Finally, the merry-go-round started to slow down and then stopped. Mother waved to me to catch my attention because I looked around and could not see her. After I saw mother I ran to her almost crying. She hugged and comforted me, seeing how scared I was to lose her.

We continued our walk to auntie's home. She and her family lived in a very big apartment house, a kind of building I had never seen in our city. My two cousins were already big girls. They kissed me and asked my name. Then they helped me to take my poor wardrobe from the suitcase and put the garments into a drawer. My auntie asked my mother, "Where are her good shoes?" My mother pointed to the sandals I was wearing.

"But those are a pair of new sandals! I just bought them last week," she said.

"I'm not taking her without black patent-leather shoes," declared my auntie. So, to my delight, I got another pair of new shoes. Usually, I got new ones only when my toes were already showing through. Later Auntie Cili sewed me a green silk dress from one of her daughters' old dresses. I felt so elegant in my new dress and shoes.

One night my cousins took me to a movie. It would have been my very first but unfortunately no children were allowed to go in. "You just stay out in the lobby until we get out. And don't you dare wander away!" my cousin told me. I still remember how bored and frightened I was to have to sit in one place for two whole hours.

Mother was already gone and I was very much alone. I went around in the big building looking for some company. Two floors above us I saw a girl no bigger than me. She was playing with her doll in an open doorway. I stood there watching the girl undress her baby preparing her for a nap. The girl looked up and smiled at me. "What is your name?" she asked.

"Ibi," I said. She asked me if I lived in the building.

"No, I am just visiting my auntie. What is your name?"

"My name is Klara," she answered. "Would you like to

hold my baby?" I held out my arms to receive the doll. I hugged her closely and kissed her on the cheek. Klara and I became friends and my happiest moments were when she let me play with her doll.

On another occasion mother took me to auntie Matilda. She lived in a smaller town but also quite far from our city. When mother left me there I was so miserable. Auntie was very strict about eating. I had to eat everything, like it or not. Some of her cooking was very spicy. She had a tailor shop in her home and after her husband's death she ran the shop with four or five assistants. One day auntie made a salad between meals from raw sliced cucumber with sour cream on top. I tasted it and it tasted awful. I made a grimace which one of the helpers saw and he suggested that I dig a hole in the garden and bury the salad. I did as I was told and took the empty bowl back to auntie. However, it was too soon. "You already finished it? You must like it very much," said my auntie. Bumm! Another portion went into the bowl.

Auntie also had a peasant girl as a housemaid. Once I complained to her about auntie and told her that I didn't like my auntie. She told on me and the next day auntie packed my things and without notifying my parents she put me on a train headed back home. I was only eight years old. It was a Sunday afternoon when I arrived and nobody was home. I climbed through the low window of our family house and went to bed. When the family returned, mother almost had a heart attack when I sat up in my bed and said, "I am home, mother."

The storm

There was an incident which I remember only because of the stories told by my parents. Our whole city was built on the lower hill of the wonderful mountain Mecsek. In the middle of our street there was a stream coming through a tunnel from the mountain. In dry weather the stream was narrow and, for us children, very enjoyable. We took off our shoes and walked in the water for about a block down and back. But you should have seen it when there was a storm! The narrow stream grew so wide that it covered the sidewalk on both sides of the street and sometimes even reached the base of the houses. At the end of the street the water went into another tunnel which was covered with an iron grate. However, the grate was wide enough that a small child could have been swept into the tunnel. Since the whole city was on a downhill slope water ran everywhere when there was a heavy rainfall.

It was a rainy day but it wasn't very bad until about four o'clock in the afternoon. The children had just started to come out of school when the rain started to become heavier by the minute. My sister, Aranka, left the grade one classroom. Most of the time mother let her come home alone because the school wasn't very far from our home. But in bad weather mother would fetch my sister. Somehow they missed each other and mother went home hoping that Aranka would get home by herself. But Aranka was not yet home when mother arrived. She rushed out frantically again looking for her child but she was nowhere in sight. The rain was very heavy and the streets were covered with thick, yellowish water. "Oh my God, where is my little girl?" mother was desperately asking. She went neighbour to neighbour but nobody knew about Aranka. Then she went to the police station where she was promised that action would be taken to find the child. We had no telephones in our homes, only a few of the privileged had them, and no cars, only public transportation or ambulances.

When my father came home at supper time there was no supper and mother was crying and the rest of the girls were very quiet. Father stepped into the kitchen and asked nervously, "What happened? Why is everybody so quiet?"

"Aranka is not home yet," said mother sobbing. My father, without another word, put his coat back on and went out. For an hour he marched around the streets which were quiet and without people by now. An hour later he arrived back home carrying something in his arms that looked like a bunch of wet rags. It was Aranka, wrapped in the wet coat, her face white as chalk. Only the frightened eyes showed that she was alive. "Where did you find her?" mother asked as she took off the child's wet clothes and wrapped her in a blanket. But father was too exhausted to explain just yet. He sat at the table, his head resting on his arms.

After he calmed down my father told the story of how he found her. She was swept away by the water as she tried to cross the road. She was pushed to the tunnel down the street and she grabbed one of the rails and hung onto it. Aranka must have had to use all her energy to hang on until the rain and the stream quieted down and there was no more danger of her being swept into the tunnel. When Aranka saw her father approaching the tunnel she cried out, "Father, father, I am here!" That was how my father saved my sister.

Unfortunately, Margaret and mother had not been on speaking terms for years. After her marriage when Margaret came to the city to see our father in his shop mother, who was there most of the day, walked out when she saw Margaret. Mother must have been so terribly hurt by Margaret's behaviour during the time she was home that she still didn't want to see her after all those years. Despite all this we girls went to visit Margaret in the little village where she lived with her husband. The place was so small it had only one general store which was owned by my brother-in-law. During my visits as a little girl, I liked to help out in the store. I learned how to make a cone-shaped bag out of a piece of paper and pour the merchandise, like a few dekagrams of salt, red pepper, yeast or other things, into it. I also liked to be there because I had the privilege of opening the big glass jars and digging into them for candies or chocolate bonbons.

I played with the peasant girls and liked the life of the village but not for very long. Later, when I grew older, I often thought about my sister, who was a city girl, and how she buried herself so young in a place where she had no friends, no entertainment, actually nothing to do. Their home was only one room and a kitchen which were spotlessly clean. There was no running water and no toilet. They had to carry buckets of water from the well in the yard. The toilet was in the back of the yard. It was a deep hole in the ground. Around it was a half meter wooden platform with a hole on top which served as the toilet seat. There was also a wooden wall around the platform with a door.

Our father went to visit his oldest daughter often on weekends, but mother was never invited. Not long ago, looking through my old photographs I found a picture of my father. It was sent to Margaret as a postcard with a message on the back written by me in 1933. The message says, "Father sends his picture to you and he also wants to inform you that he will go to see you on Saturday night. I'll also visit you on Friday morning. We both send our love. Ibi"

In the photograph father is standing in front of his shop on one of the three steps. He wears his working clothes, a pair of worn out pants, a flannelette shirt and a sweater. His white hair is covered with a cap. On both sides of the door there are some cans, buckets, and a couple of dishes for milking cows. On the left side of the door on the outside wall is an inscription which says he will fix, at low cost, plumbing and old and worn out household items.

After many years of Margaret and mother not speaking to each other my sister Aranka finally made peace between them. It happened during one of Margaret's visits to see our father in his shop. Aranka, who was then about 16 years old also was in the shop. When Margaret entered my mother, as usual, got up to leave. But Aranka gently pushed mother back onto her seat and then turned to Margaret and asked, "Don't you think it is time to ask mother's forgiveness" Then she said to mother, "And you, mother, have to accept Margaret's apology no matter what has happened in the past."

For a few minutes Margaret just stood there not knowing what to say. Finally, she went over to mother and said, "Forgive me, mother, what I have done to you but I was just a little girl and I missed my own mother very much. I was angry with father for having a new wife. I didn't want a new mother! I was told by every one that stepmothers are bad. Now I know that you are not." Before mother could open her mouth Margaret grabbed her hand and kissed it. This gesture made mother so pleased that she stood up and hugged Margaret. Aranka was very happy that she was able to make peace between her sister and her mother.

Ilona, my other step-sister, also married. She moved to a fairly big city with her husband. She was also twenty years old when she married. Her husband, Leslie, was twenty-five. He worked as a clerk in an insurance company. Their son, George, was born the following year, in 1926. Elizabeth and I took turns visiting them and we loved to babysit for our little nephew. Baja was a few hours by train from Pécs. Unlike Pécs, Baja had a river, the Sugovica, which ran into the Danube River. The banks of the Sugovica were a favourite beach for the locals. I remember on a summer morning, my brother-in-law rented a boat and Ilona, her baby son, Ilona's girlfriend Irene and I went for a boat ride. Only Leslie knew how to row the boat. A huge ship was standing not far from the shore, its engine ready to go. As my brother-in-law rowed our boat, it went dangerously close to the ship and almost drifted under it. I saw Leslie's dead white and perspiring face as he used all his energy to get away from the ship. Finally he succeeded. I wasn't aware of the danger. Only later did I hear Irene say to Leslie that she knew how close we all were to drowning.

My teenhood to my marriage

After I finished the Jewish Elementary School in 1926 I was enrolled in the state public school. I wasn't the best student but I was good in subjects that I liked, or if I liked the teacher who taught them. One of my favourite subject was natural science, maybe because I liked the teacher, Miss Ilonka, very much. I also wasn't too bad in German because I had always wanted to learn a second language. My mother was too busy to see if we did our homework. Sometimes she came into the room to see what I was doing and was satisfied when she saw that I was studying. But I wasn't. I would put a fiction book on top of my schoolbook and pretend.

In school I made some friends and the humiliations and mocking that I had received in elementary school were over. But they had left scars. There are two incidents which are vivid in my memory today. I was in the third grade of this school, twelve or thirteen years old. One day our German teacher announced; "Girls, tomorrow there is going to be an exam. You better look through last month's lessons."

Next morning when she told us what the exam would be, I was glad because I had studied it beforehand and knew it well and by heart. During the exam the teacher, Miss Gertrude, collected the work from those who were finished while the others were still writing. I was finished early and had done an excellent job. My teacher took it but in a few minutes she returned, threw my work on my desk with big red letters on it, "Copied!" It came to me like a bolt of lightening from a sunny sky. "You copied the whole thing from your neighbour," Miss Gertrude said. I knew that I was innocent and I screamed at the top of my voice denying the accusation.

"No! No! I didn't copy. I knew it by heart. I studied that piece and I knew it well." I was so upset and I cried so hard in a way that I wouldn't be able to do if I had been guilty. I thought I was going to faint. Finally, the teacher let me go to her desk on the platform and re-write the whole exam. Of course I couldn't do it as well as before. I made some errors and she gave me a mark of three. The best mark was a number one and the worst, which was a five, was a failure. Without her accusation I would have gotten the best mark. However, in the other episode I have to confess that I was the guilty one. Our mathematics teacher was an elderly woman with very bad eyesight. The students knew it, and many of them took advantage of it. When we had homework we had to place it on the edge of our desk and the teacher took a glance at each person's work but she really didn't see it. Occasionally she lifted some of the notebooks to have a closer look. Many times when the girls didn't do their homework they would just put out their work from the day before. I had never dared to do it but it happened that once I forgot my homework so I did what many girls had done before, and placed my former day's work on my desk. The unexpected happened. Miss Irma, our teacher, lifted my notebook close to her eyes and saw my cheating. She asked the girls if anyone had a pin. Guess what? My best friend offered a pin and the teacher pinned my notebook on my back and sent me to the corner facing the wall.

Oh, how embarassed I was! I knew that I was guilty but why did she notice me on my first attempt when so many of the girls got away with it? And why had my best friend offered that damn pin!

After I finished the state public school mother asked me what I wanted to do. I could go on for further education like Aranka, who went to business school for a couple of years and became a secretary in a law office, or I could begin as an apprentice in a dressmaker's shop. I chose the latter. For one and one half years I learned the trade. The first six months I did everything but sew. I had to babysit, dust furniture, and do other household chores. I graduated from sewing after the year and a half but I never became a dressmaker. I never liked it very much and I didn't have the talent to be a good one. Or maybe I remembered what the boss's domestic help once told me, "Ibi, you will never become a dressmaker." I worked for a few more years and got a small salary.

Aranka was nineteen and engaged when another accident happened to her. One day her boss asked her to fetch some papers from City Hall. It was late, near closing time, so she had to hurry. Putting on her coat hastily it caught in her shoe-heel and the hemline was torn. There was no time to sew it back so Aranka pinned it up with a needle. Then she forgot the whole incident until next morning when she put her coat on again to go to work. As she put her arms into the coat's sleeves and jerked the coat up on her back the pin stuck and broke into her calf. "Mother!" she screamed, "A needle has broken into my calf!" Unbelieving, mother looked for the needle and found only half of it on the floor. The other half had disappeared into Aranka's flesh. They went to the nearest hospital and an x-ray showed the half needle. But by the time the doctor took her to the operating room the piece of heedle had moved away. Finally, right there under the x-ray machine, they removed the needle and my sister was sent home.

The next morning, however, she became very feverish and her leg swelled to double its usual size. Mother took Aranka back to the hospital and this time they admitted her. The infection moved higher every day and pus reached her thigh. There was no penicillin at that time and doctors gave her as much medicine as she could bear. Finally, as a last solution, the doctors decided to amputate her leg. My parents had already signed the papers to save their child's life. Aranka cried out "No! I won't let them! I'd rather die! Mother, don't allow it. Please, mother, tell the doctors to save my leg!"

Aranka had already returned her engagement ring but her fiance put it back on her finger saying: "They are not going to amputate your leg. You are going to be allright. You will see."

The doctors were moved by my sister's plea and waited a couple of days more. They gave Aranka as much medication as she possibly could take. Then a miracle, and doctors usually don't believe in miracles, happened. The pus, which was up in her thigh, slowly started to recede. When her fiance heard the good news he said to her, "You see, my dear, I told you that you were going to be allright." But he admitted to us that he hadn't believed his own words. After about four weeks, Aranka was finally free of infection and fever. I saw her in the hospital, very thin and weak, walking slowly down the corridor aided by two nurses. They actually taught her to walk again.

I was fifteen years old when I joined a Zionist group. I was very active in it and even wrote small articles in our monthly paper. We talked about many topics, read Darwin and Freud and learned the Hebrew language. Actually, we were completely prepared for a kibbutz life in Israel, which was then called Palestine. I very much enjoyed being in that group. We went for excursions in our wonderful mountains. I had always liked nature. I marvelled at the huge pine trees, colourful wild flowers, prattling little streams and the songs of different birds. I could listen for hours to birds as they answered each others' calls.

My best memories were when our group went for a camping trip. It took a while to convince my parents to let me go. The campsite was near the border of Czechoslovakia. The mountains, called Matra, were famous for their beauty and natural hot springs. We had so much fun in the camp. We played games and football with the boys. Almost every night we built a campfire and sat around having a good time. We entertained ourselves by reading poems, making small plays or just singing the sad melodies of beautiful Hebrew songs. We slept in tents on straw matresses. The boys' tents were separated from those of the girls. Our counsellors were responsible young adults.

The boys always made jokes about us girls. I still remember one night when two of the boys came into our tent. Since they believed that I was sleeping they pulled my matress outside, with me on it. I pretended not to awaken so as not to spoil their fun. But at other times, fortunately, the joke was not on me; the boys painted some of the girls' faces with black shoe polish.

To my sorrow our three weeks of camping came to an end. We were saying our farewells sitting together around the fire, sipping our tea, eating the cookies, talking and singing. In the camp we had gathered from many cities in Hungary. A boy, who had come a little later to the campfire, sat beside me. I had seen him many times before and liked him a lot, but he was surrounded constantly by girls and he didn't even know I existed, or so I thought. He was very handsome. Tall, slim with wavy brown hair and brown eyes. Only his nose was a bit prominent in his narrow face but I liked that too. I felt lucky that the handsome one had sat beside me. He introduced himself as Zoltan, Zolti for short, and asked what my name was. He came from another city and was eighteen years old. We talked about our cities, about books, movies we had seen and other subjects. Before the end of the night we exchanged addresses. We corresponded for years.

I had a few girlfriends from school who had also joined the Zionist movement. I still treasure a picture from that time that shows me with my girlfriends in uniform. We wore navy blue skirts, grey cotton blouses and royal blue triangle neckties. My friends' names, as recorded on the back of the picture, were Lily Neuman, Piri Schlanger, Gizi Stern and myself, Ibi Szalai. My best friend was Gizi. She also had a boyfriend from another city and they also corresponded with each other.

Gizi and I spent many evenings together in our home. We made the night romantic by putting the light out and opening the ceramic stove's outer door so that we could see only the wood glowing in the dark. We talked about our wishes, dreams, and boys, and we read the letters from our boyfriends to each other. Occasionally I met other boys from the group. I especially remember one of them.

One hot summer day he escorted me home. He was a medical student in university. Mother called him in and asked, "-Would you like some cold watermelon?"

"Yes, Aunt Szalai. Thank you," he answered. He won my mother's heart immediately with his simple words spoken without any reluctance. Mother was only sorry that I didn't like Sandor because of the pimples on his face.

During the almost two years I corresponded with Zolti we came to know and love each other through long, monthly letters. In our letters we recorded everything that had happened in our young lives. If I saw a good movie I wrote down its content. I also wrote about the books I read and often we exchanged our opinions or even argued about it in our letters.

Zolti often wrote that I was smart, intelligent, pretty and that he was in love with me. I built up my self-confidence — lacking before that — tremendously. We fell deeper and deeper in love. He was my whole world. He visited me a few times and my parents liked him too. Zolti was an only child. His parents were poor and they wanted a rich girl for their son. They were very much opposed to our friendship.

I try to recall my feelings from those years. Both my sisters, Aranka and Elizabeth, were very good in some sports, especially in swimming. They were also good dancers. I remember Aranka's enrollment in dance classes when she was fifteen or sixteen. She danced beautifully and she always had a marvelous time in the classes or at an occasional ballroom dance. When Elizabeth and I reached that age we went to those classes also. While Elizabeth was also very good and fast to learn to dance, somehow it was difficult for me and I never learned to dance well. Most of the time I sat through dances. The fact that I was the prettiest of the three didn't help much. I wasn't a good dancer and that was it. Finally, I quit the classes altogether. I felt that I was a failure in everything. It seemed that the humiliation and mockery I had received as a child in school had left their marks.

When Zolti's letters started to come more infrequently and finally stopped, I was devastated. I became more and more withdrawn every day. I had lost interest in everything. Mother took me to a doctor and he said that I was under tremendous stress and he advised me to go to a hospital for some medication and rest. In the hospital I wanted to be left alone and I didn't want to see anybody from my family, not even my mother. Yet I loved my parents, they had never abused me but they were very busy making a living and they hadn't time for me. Shortly I felt better and I was discharged from the hospital. Now the doctor suggested that a change in my environment would be most helpful. Mother wrote my sister, Aranka, to ask that she take me in for a short time and find a job for me. Aranka had already been married for a couple of years and lived in Budapest with her husband.

I had not heard from Zolti for all this time. It hurt me very much still, I was only 19 years old and he was my first and only love from the age of fifteen. I was sure that his parents had forbidden him to see me or to write to me. I tried not to think of my sweetheart any more.

Aranka and her husband, Jeno, took me to their home for the sake of our mother. Jeno got a job for me in a thread factory where I worked ten hours a day. At first, my life was very simple. After work, having stood on my feet for those long hours, I went home dead tired. After supper, I washed myself and went to bed and early next morning I started my daily routine again. This continued for some time. I was quiet and withdrawn for a while but gradually I started to talk with my colleagues and to read books on weekends. I had always liked to read and now sitting in the corner of the couch with a good book became my favourite pastime again. I especially remember one novel, Margaret Mitchell's *Gone With the Wind* in an Hungarian translation.

One day I opened a drawer in my sister's kitchen and found an open envelope with a letter inside addressed to me. It was Zolti's handwriting. My sister had hidden it from me. Maybe she meant well, but she didn't know how every day I was waiting for a word, a message, a hint from him. I wanted to forget him but I couldn't. And here was letter from him that hadn't been given to me! With shaking hands I took the letter out of the envelope and started to read while tears gathered in my eyes. I had to stop a few times to wipe away my tears. Zolti wrote that he had gotten my address from my parents and that he still loved me! He had heard that I was sick and felt responsible for it. Soon he would come to Budapest and would like to see me. I was in seventh heaven after reading these words!

After five or six weeks I moved out of my sister's place and rented a bed from a single elderly lady who also provided meals for a reasonable price. But I didn't stay there very long either. I had made friends with a girl who was also alone and only a couple of years older than I and we decided to move in together. This move was good for both of us. We shared our expenses and we also became good companions. My new friend, Babus, was a little on the chubby side and a few inches taller than I. I still remember very well her big, beautiful blue eyes. Her hair was naturally curly and blond in contrast to mine. It was a nice summer day, Babus had a date and I was alone at home in the little garden behind the house reading a book, resting on a lounge chair. My hair was in rollers drying under the sun. Suddenly I had a feeling that somebody was watching me. I looked up and there was Zolti, standing a few feet away, looking down at me. There is no word to describe the surprise and joy I felt at that moment. He came over, helped me from the chair and hugged me. We clung to each other, tears pouring down our faces. He was not ashamed to show his feelings and his tears. "You love me! You still love me!" I repeated over and over.

Even now, tears well into my eyes as I write about that meeting. I love him with every beat of my heart. I always did and I always will! When I thought that I had lost him and tried to accept it he came back! "We belong together darling!" he said. "I'll never leave you again."

Zolti told me that he had had a fight with his parents over me. He left his home town Papa, and was now also working in Budapest. During the summer we dated as much as we could. Our salary was only enough for everyday living and very seldom could we afford a luxury like a movie, a glass of beer, or a cup of *espresso*, which he liked. But we were happy without any extras. We went to the beach, to museums, or window-shopping, which were all free. Occasionally we went to a restaurant to eat a cheap meal. We took long walks hand in hand and we were happy! Very happy! I still lived with my roommate and Zolti rented a room with another boy.

Zolti's parents

Soon after Zolti came to Budapest, his parents also moved there from their city, Papa. I think it was 1938. Zolti made up with his parents but as far as I knew he didn't speak to them about me. However, one day he announced, "Dress up nicely, darling. We are going to see my parents. I want them to know you." I was very excited.

"What will I tell them? Will they like me? How do I look?" I showered him with questions.

"Just be yourself. You are O.K. You are pretty," Zolti said. I was very nervous when we arrived at his parents' home at 16 Nepszinhaz Street. His mother was kind and friendly to me. I resembled her a little bit. She was short like me, with dark hair and brown eyes. Her face was round and her long hair was in two braids wrapped around the crown of her head. She was a simple but good-hearted person with not much education but with a natural brightness. She dressed very simply and absolutely refused to wear a hat. Zolti's father was a very handsome, tall man like his son, but he had blue eyes and light hair. He wore eyeglasses. His nose was slightly turned up which made his looks more gentile than Jewish. He looked very distinguished. He was educated and intelligent. Somehow I had the feeling that they were not a perfect match but they had a good marriage. He liked to dress elegantly and he was very neat and clean. They welcomed me into the family. Zolti's father said that though it was true that I didn't have any dowry and I was not rich, I did have a job and I was a diligent worker.

They both agreed to our marriage which we planned to take place in the near future. But first we wanted to visit my parents in Pécs. In those years there was a so-called penny express which meant that for less than half price people could go from Budapest to some bigger cities for a day. We bought two tickets and on a Sunday, early in the morning, we met in the West railway station. Zolti surprised me, wearing a new grey-striped suit which he bought for this occasion. He was so handsome and I was so proud of him! My parents were terribly happy for me and they took my Zolti into their heart. We had only one day but I even had some time to go and introduce my fiance to my girlfriends. My younger sister Elizabeth who just got married and lived with her in-laws came home with her new husband to be with us on this special day.

Mother prepared a lovely lunch which we ate outdoors in the little courtyard among the colourful and fragrant flowers. Oh, how happy I was among my loved ones! Involuntarily I thought back to the time when not long ago I was so miserable and so devastated at home that I never thought that it would be over some day and that I would be happy again!

That day was over very soon and at night everybody escorted us to the railway station to say good-bye. Back in Budapest, when Zolti had saved enough money he bought an engagement ring for me which was also a wedding band. It was not traditional to buy separate rings for engagements and weddings. Instead, during the engagement the bride-to-be wore the ring on her left hand's ring-finger and after the wedding moved the ring to the right hand. I remember after we had purchased the ring and were showing it to Zolti's mother it fell to the floor and rolled away. "Bad luck," my future mother-in-law said.

We were engaged for about a year and we married in the fall of 1939, on the threshold of war. My parents went into debt to give me a bedroom set like all the other four girls had received. My father came to the wedding, which was very simple. Mother was so sick she couldn't come. We didn't even have enough money for a wedding dress and Zolti borrowed an overcoat from his friend. I had a navy-blue pleated skirt, a white blouse and a three quarter length navy-blue coat. I wore a little white hat with veil and a pair of navy-blue shoes. Father was very proud when he overheard somebody say, "The bride is very pretty."

My in-laws gave us just enough money to go to a nice restaurant and to a hotel for our wedding night. We couldn't afford an apartment so we shared my in-laws' two-bedroom apartment. Two bedroom then meant two rooms only and a kitchen and a toilet. We didn't even have a bathroom. One of the rooms was rented to a young couple, so we put a double bed in the kitchen and that was our bedroom until the tenants moved out.

I had a steady job in the thread factory where I worked in shifts either from six in the morning to two in the afternoon or from two to ten in the evening. Some days we could only meet late at night. Those times I wrote little notes like, "Be careful I just washed the floor."

Zolti answered on the paper, "I was careful." Zolti's trade was that of a mechanic for fine instruments like sewing machines and radios. He also mastered chiropody and massage. He preferred to work at the latter and he worked in spas of which there were many in Budapest. My father-in-law also worked in thermal spas and his name was well known because of his good and conscientious work with his patients. Later, when he was not allowed to work in the spas, my father-in-law worked at home. He made two compartments with curtains around them in their room. He had many patients. My mother-in-law did the cooking during all the time while we were together. After about six months Zolti and I moved into the inner room. Before that we went to buy furniture from the money father left us. We bought a combination of bedroom and living room all in one. There was a divan which we would open at night for sleeping, a small round table with two armchairs, an end table with a night-lamp and a big wardrobe. In the middle of the wardrobe was a small china cabinet, one side was for the dresses and suits, the other side was for linen and lingerie, and there were three drawers for other things. I made curtains and table cloths from lace, white for the windows and gold for the table. Every little piece we got or bought was a treasure for us. I made our room friendly and cosy.

Our entertainment was a movie or very seldom a theatre. Sometimes we played a game of "Monopoly" with our friends. Zolti's favourite actor was Fred Astair and we saw every one of his films. Arriving home he copied those tap dances very well. In the summertime we went to beaches or strolled on the bank of our river Danube or window shopped in the elegant boutiques. To buy some necessity like a pair of shoes or dress or suit was a big event. Once I lost a pair of leather gloves and I couldn't get over it for days.

Zolti had a little simple camera and he took nice photographs. His wish was to have a better camera. So he saved from penny to penny and finally he had enough. But shopping for the camera wasn't very simple. We went to shop from one side of the street to the other until he got what he wanted for a reasonable price. Finally he bought it and after we got out of the store he grabbed me and kissed me all over my face. "What was all this kissing for?" I asked him. "Because you let me buy it," he said and he was very happy. I saved this camera through the war but it was stolen later in Israel.

My motherhood

Mama and papa, as I called my in-laws, were good to us. It was a cold winter day in 1941 when Zolti and I went to a doctor. I suspected that I was pregnant. Because of the war, we didn't plan to have any children. When the doctor confirmed that I was three months pregnant I went out crying from the doctor's office into my husband's open arms. I was frightened and confused when I told him the news. Those were uncertain times and I wondered about the future: what could it hold for a Jewish child? But I remember well my husband's words, "Don't cry, darling, we need this baby, you will see." My dearest didn't know how true those words were. Later, when I calmed down, like most mothers-to-be I had many questions. Would the baby be a boy or a girl? Who would it resemble? I was healthy and strong and worked almost to the end of my pregnancy. My in-laws were happy and mama said when I told her of my doubt, "If God gave lamb he will certainly give pasture ground." I started to sew baby things and Zolti made a shelf for the baby's clothes. From time to time I took them out and imagined my baby in them. By the time my child's birthday arrived the hatred for us Jews was getting worse.

It was a hot summer night on 16 July 1942 when I was awakened by my labour pains. I turned on the light on the end table and saw the clock showed four in the morning. I didn't want to wake Zolti so I waited a couple of hours and the pains stopped. My husband went to work because I insisted but later in the morning the pains started again. I told mama they were coming every ten minutes or so. She calmly took out the wooden tub we used for washing clothes and taking baths. She gave me a bath and helped me to get dressed. The clinic where I had to go for monthly check-ups and lectures for baby care was just walking distance away. Mama escorted me there but to my surprise the hospital staff said that there was no bed for me. It was suggested that I could either lie on the floor or go somewhere else. Since this was the clinic which I had visited during my pregnancy and my pains were getting stronger, I agreed to stay on the floor. But I didn't have to. I got a bed after all. It seemed that clinic's intention was to make things difficult because I was a Jew.

About two p.m. my pains were so strong that they took me into the delivery room. When Zolti telephoned, he was told not to come because they didn't expect the baby to be born until the next day. On the wall across from my stretcher was a big round clock. I was watching it so that is how I know that my son was born a few minutes after five p.m. on the same day. I was too excited to eat anything the whole day, therefore I was very hungry after the delivery. It took a very long time before I was given a glass of milk. Only after many hours did I receive the required attention. I was wheeled to a corridor and left there for hours. I hoped that they were providing my baby with better, proper care. The very next day my husband and his parents came to visit. Zolti lovingly held the baby's tiny fingers and said how beautiful and perfect his son was. He already talked about how we would raise our son to be a sportsman like his daddy.

The atmosphere in the hospital was terrible. It was 1942 and war was everywhere in Europe. Although war came to Hungary a little later the hatred of the Jews was already evident. There were no separate rooms for the babies. Each lay in a little basket at the foot of their mother's bed. One day a mother screamed for the help of a doctor when checking her baby she saw her infant had vomited blood. When the doctor came running the nurse in charge said to him, "Don't run, doctor, it is only a Jewish bastard."

I was happy that within five days I could leave the hospital. Zolti bought a second-hand baby carriage. He cleaned and polished it and it looked like new when I got home. We were happy and proud of our little son. It was so good to hold him in my arms. I wished that I could protect him from every bad thing that might come. Unfortunately, I could not protect him for very long. My son, Andy, was four months old when his father was taken away to a labour camp. Zolti was allowed visiting days only once every couple of months to see his family. Zolti was so caring and protective to the child during those short months he could see him. Andy was about eighteen months old when his father saw him for the last time. He already could say "daddy Zolti" in his special baby-talk. I recall one episode vividly. Andy was seven or eight months old and as I held him in my arms, he hit my face. Of course, as a baby he didn't know what he was doing. But Zolti, who was home on leave, gently took the baby's hand and said, "Never ever hit your mother — not even as a baby."

My in-laws adored the child and they wanted me to stay home to take care of him. Our apartment was unhealthy because it was on the street level of a seven-storey building. It was dark and damp. I took Andy to the nearby park every day and spent many hours there with him. By this time my younger sister Elizabeth was also married and had moved to Budapest. Aranka's only child, Marianna, was seven years old when Andy was born.

In the late spring of 1943 I decided to take Andy to see my parents in Pécs. They had sold the family house and rented a one-bedroom apartment near their shop. My son was ten months old when I took him to my parents. He was their third grandchild. The first had been Ilona's son George, born in 1926. Margaret and Elizabeth had no children.

My parents were very happy to see us and to meet the new baby. Mother was happiest when she took the baby for a stroll in his stroller. She would babysit when my father and I went to a movie. Father liked movies very much. Father built a small crib for the child, so my worry about where the baby would sleep was solved. My parents had a little better life now that all their daughters were out of the house and married. My visit with them was almost over when one early morning there was a knock on the door and my Zolti walked in as a surprise. He stayed a day or two and then we went home together. That was the last time that I saw my parents.

My husband had been sent home from the camp and told he could stay for a while. Somehow we hadn't paid much attention to what had been happening for years everywhere in Europe. We were young and optimistic, hoping that the terrible things would not happen to us. Hungary, and especially Budapest, were the last to be occupied by the Germans.

War in Hungary

Then it happened. On 19 March 1944 the Germans invaded Hungary. After that, bad events happened very quickly every day. Destructive laws for Jews came into force. We were not allowed to go to any public places, like cinemas or restaurants. We had to surrender our radios to the government. Only at certain times of the day could we go out to buy food or go to the park. On the streetcars we could sit only at the back of the vehicle. On 6 April of the same year every Jew from the age of six had to put the yellow star on his or her chest. All men from the age of 18 to 60 were called into labour camps which had already become concentration camps. Zolti and his father were also taken away. Later the women from age 18 to 50 had to go.

There were houses in some districts appointed "Jewish Houses" with huge yellow stars on their fronts. Our building became one, we could stay in our home but we had to take other Jewish people in. My husband's two female cousins moved in with us. A ghetto was formed in the heart of the city.

On our street was a nice little pastry shop and the owner was friendly and adored my baby. As I was not allowed to go in, I used to write a note and give it with some money to my son, saying, "Be careful, sweetheart, hold the money tight, give it to the lady and she will give you your favourite *torte*. You are a big boy and I am going to let you go in alone and wait for you outside." He got his pastry and the lady escorted my child back to me with a kiss on his cheek. Another time we were riding on a streetcar and because our time to be out on the street was over I didn't wear the yellow star.

Suddenly in the quiet vehicle my son's lisping voice was heard, "Mommy, where is your yellow star?" Fortunately, only I could understand my baby's question.

Without answering him I said quickly, pointing through the window, "Look at those big trucks with many soldiers on them." Andy was satisfied and didn't demand an answer. If any of our fellow Hungarians had understood the child's question, we would have been in big trouble.

My sister Aranka's bungalow in the outskirts of the city was also appointed a so-called "Jewish House." She took our sister Elizabeth in and also some friends with their family. After October 1944 our communication stopped and I didn't know what happened to them until after our liberation.

What happened from that point on is described in a letter I wrote on 30 January 1945, only two weeks after our liberation from the ghetto. The purpose of my letter was to write down what had happened to us while it was fresh in my memory, and give it to Zolti who I was sure would come out of that hell alive. I still have the original letter written with pencil by a single candle light, the pages now yellowed with time and the words faded away.

Budapest, Jan. 30th 1945

My dearest love!

Nine months ago, on the 9th of May in 1944 when you kissed me good-bye, I told you my life would be worthless if you did not come back. "I will be back, sweetheart, because I love you and our little son. Don't worry, my dear," you replied to me. Now we are home and safe and so are your parents, and I feel that you will come home too. I feel it very strongly! Our little son prays for you every night with his tiny hands clasped together.

Where should I begin to tell you of our sufferings? I want to tell you everything that has happened to us. Maybe I'll go back to the 15th of October 1944. Our Regent, Horthy, spoke on the radio and we were told that Hungary would not fight, nobody had to worry. We were tremendously glad to hear it. We all crowded to the yard of our building to hear the declaration of our regent from the janitor's radio. We were jumping with joy and tearing off the yellow stars from our chests. We thought it was the end of our sufferings. We had had enough. For example, the yellow stars which discriminate us from other citizens, we were not allowed to go out of the house except between five and seven in the evening to buy groceries, of course by that time there were not many groceries left. We were forbidden to go to any public places like cafeterias, soda shops, movies or playgrounds. On the streetcars or buses we could only sit at the back. In many of the stores you could read this "Dogs and Jews forbidden to enter!" There were many other awful things but now we thought that an end had finally come to these orders. We were wrong. Even more bad things started. Our regent had the best intentions but he was weak and on the same day the Arrow Cross Party, with its leader Szalasi Ferencz, took over the presidency. Szalasi was bloodthirsty. He swore that he would help the Germans to exterminate the Jews.

The next morning I saw sixty or more people — men, women and children — marching with their hands raised above their heads. Fascists escorted them. Later on the same day, some police and fascists with swastikas on their arms came to our building. One of them roared, "Every Jew down to the yard or I shoot!" We were very scared. You know, dear, by then about three hundred people lived in the building, most of them Jews. We had no time to pack anything. I just grabbed the knapsack, little Andy's winter coat, and a blanket. Those things were always ready in case of an air-raid. We had to raise our hands like criminals and form a double line in front of the house. When Andy heard those words "hands up" he took his hand out of mine and raised his too.

First they took us to the nearest open ground and robbed us. Money, wristwatches, rings, flashlights; we had to throw them all on a blanket. We had to put our hands up again so they could inspect if any rings were left. If they found something, they beat our hands with a whip. I put my wedding band in Andy's coat pocket. I wanted to save it.

While we were marching with raised hands to the open ground to be robbed you couldn't imagine what the crowd on the street did to us. They were standing along the sidewalk enjoying our march. They hit and spat on us. One man grabbed the blanket from my hand, so Andy had no cover for the night. Others took the coats off of people's shoulders. One man beat your father and smashed his eyeglasses. After we were robbed we were ordered to form a double line once more and to march to an unknown place. At that point Andy and I lost your parents in the crowd. On the route I saw that we were being led to the Tattersal racetrack. There we spent two horrible days and nights. It was like a nightmare. When we arrived it was already dark. We had to sit down on the bare ground which was covered with dung from the horses. There were a lot of people because they had been collected from every part of the city. Many of them didn't have even a place to sit so they stood all night. The children fell asleep in their mothers' laps. Andy too fell asleep and I hugged him in my lap all night to keep him warm. We adults were awake the whole night waiting for the morning. What would happen to us? Finally, morning came. We were ordered once more to form in a line of four and to walk around a platform where some Arrow Cross bandits were standing with machine guns in their hands, pointing at us. One of them roared, "You rotten Jews! All of you will die within a few hours." But nothing had happened yet except that we had no food, water, or roof above our heads.

During the day we walked all over the place looking for mama and papa. There were Arrow Cross women with whips and they hit everybody around them. I tried to avoid those beasts. From time to time Andy and I sat down on the ground and I fed him some crackers and apples from the knapsack. I couldn't take a bite. After that we again went to look for your parents. Finally in mid-afternoon we found each other. We were crying and hugging to try to comfort each other. We all sat down on the ground again to try to keep Andy warm. Then came the second night. About three a.m. we suddenly saw a bright light and a man on a loudspeaker announced that we could all go home. The order came from the chief Szalasi, who had become the head of the government. As soon as we got out, German soldiers shot among us at random. Many were wounded and killed, but somehow we got home. Little Andy's first words were "Hello, my red tricycle you say hello to me too." You know dear, he had just received that red tricycle from uncle Joe, our superintendent, before we were taken away. He liked the child very much.

After we got home no Jews were allowed to go out on the streets for three days. Arrow Cross Party members searched us to prepare to take us to labour camps. All women up to fifty years of age and all men up to sixty were to go. I had been worried every minute of the day. I decided not to go but to hide somewhere. During the night I slept fully clothed, on top of the bed in case they came for me during the night. I had decided to hide in a closet or under the bed.

One morning soldiers and policemen came to our building with a written order that every woman between the ages of eighteen and fifty had to leave for the labour camps. We could take some food and clothes with us. We were just ready to go to the appointed place when another order came with another soldier. He said that those women whose husbands or fathers were already in a camp could stay home. You and papa were already far away so I was allowed to stay home. But not for long.

Two days later another order came saying that every woman had to go, no matter where her husband or father was. I didn't want to go but I couldn't hide either because I had no other documents but my own which said I was a Jew. Some women had false papers so they were able to hide.

Before I was ready to go I heard good news. On Columbus Street there was a Red Cross Home and children could go there to stay. The next night it was raining and about twenty-five children from the building and some mothers, myself includ-ed, went to that place. The janitor arranged for two nice police-men to escort us to prevent the crowds from lynching us. On the way I told Andy, "Darling, you will see what a nice place we are going to. There will be many little white beds for ba-bies, lots of toys, and nice nurses who will take care of you." I really meant what I told him. How could I have been so naive? The poor child was so happy to hear it that I had to tell him over and over.

By the time we arrived we were soaking wet. All the time we walked it rained very hard. There was darkness; no lights were allowed because of the air-raids. Dead people were still lying in front of the buildings on the sidewalk. We almost stepped on them. That afternoon there had been a terrible air raid with heavy bombing. Many houses were damaged with many losses. Those attacks came every day and nobody knew who would be next to die. At last we entered the Red Cross House. However, there were no little beds, nurses, food, or any lights. In the darkness we moved to the cellar which was already very crowded. I put my overcoat on the floor in a corner, took off Andy's wet shoes and coat and laid him on the floor. He fell asleep immediately. Somehow we arranged a little place for all the children to lie down.

Darling, can you imagine that in this building which was big enough for about six hundred people, there were already three thousand! And still people came. People who had escaped from camps, young and old, children without parents, babies with their mothers. There were orphans and crippled children, all of them very dirty and sick, with bugs in their hair. Children who had been well-cared for, clean and beautiful at home with their parents. But their parents had been killed or taken away to labour or concentration camps and neighbours had put the children in that home and left them there. I was lucky to be with Andy. We were there a little over two weeks. It is so hard to tell you how terrible those two weeks were. After that Andy got sick and I went home with him to mama.

One Saturday afternoon, we were sleeping when mama came into the room to wake me. Her face was pale and her hands were shaking. "Ibi, my child, you have to escape with the baby again. The policemen and Arrow Cross members are going door-to-door. They want to collect us. I don't know where they will take us. You and Andy have to escape."

I took out a suitcase put some clothes in it, among them your nice new pyjamas and shirt which I bought for you and which you liked very much. I told mama to come with us. It took some time to convince her. Finally she agreed and we went back to the Red Cross Home. A few hours later they took away all the remaining Jews from the building. The younger ones were taken to the railway station where they would be sent to camps, the older people were taken to the ghetto. I thought that no matter how awful the Red Cross Home was, at least we would be safe. Safe, but for how long?

Not very long. They had noticed that people were hiding there. I was sure we had been denounced by our fellow Hungarians. On the third of December 1944 policemen and Arrow Cross bandits who called themselves soldiers encircled the building. Once more we had to go to the yard. I saw some women lying on the ground. They had committed suicide. They had taken poison they had kept for this final use. They couldn't bear the ordeal any longer. When I saw the white foam around their mouths, I looked in the other direction. I couldn't stand the sight of them. "You should have waited for this final act," I thought. "Maybe there is still hope to live."

The same thing happened again. They robbed us of everything which had any value. I put my wedding band and some money in Andy's coat pocket again. All of us were ordered to go to a stadium where we were sorted. They made two groups. One group for the young people, another for older ones and young mothers with babies under a year of age. Andy was two years and two months old. Those little ones who were over one year had to be left behind, or strangers could take them to the ghetto.

My dear God! How terrible it was to hear the children crying for their mothers, and mothers screaming for their children. The people who did this to us had no hearts at all, only stones in their chests.

Mama and I were always at the end of the line. You remember what your mother used to say? 'Those who gain time, can save their lives.' I put a black headkerchief on my head in an attempt to hide my face. I couldn't. A policeman came over and yelled at me "Can't you hear? Are you deaf? Young ones over there!" he roared and pointed to a group. I put Andy in mama's arms.

He was screaming, "Mommy! Mommy! Don't go, don't leave me!" My heart wanted to fall apart. I told mama to come after me. It was a good idea because she met a policeman she knew from her home town. Mama begged and cried for help. Finally, the policeman pointed to the ghetto group. I took Andy in my arms and covered him with a blanket to hide both of our faces. This time I was lucky. Despite the inspections, I always turned the opposite way when the policeman passed, and nobody noticed how young I was. Then we were ordered to walk. It was a long way through the city to the ghetto. I did not dare look back. It was horrible to hear those cries and moans. I knew they were being ordered to concentration camps. Most of them died there.

I'll tell you what the ghetto was like. It was several streets downtown bounded by Kiraly Street and Dohany Street on the west and east and Karoly korut and Nagyatadi Szabo Street on the north and south. In between there were about ten streets. There was a wooden wall all around the ghetto and two gates where Arrow Cross men were standing guard. The non-Jewish population had to move out and move into abandoned Jewish homes. They had lots of choices because we were concentrated fifteen to one room. Many Jewish homes and apartments were left free.

We were taken to 45 Akacfa Street. It was dark again. We went up to the fourth floor with about thirty people. We were dead tired, not only from walking but because mama and I had taken turns carrying our sleeping Andy. We had to wait about two hours when finally the janitor opened the apartment on a police order. It was a two-room apartment. Mama, my girlfriend Mary Csillag, whom I had met on the way, and I were the first to step in. Quickly we put our children on the couch. Four people slept on that couch for seven weeks. Other people found a place for themselves on the floor or in armchairs or in the two beds in the other room.

The ghetto's gate was open until the twentieth of December. I went out a few times when I had a chance to buy or ask for some food. Some of our friends were humane and gave me what they could spare. On the twentieth of December they closed the gates. Nobody was allowed to get in or out except the driver of a hearse. I felt like a mouse in a trap.

Andy became sick again. It seemed to be pneumonia. He became pitifully thin, and there was no doctor or medicine. But God helped him. He got better. By that time we had no food. We got some meals for the first few weeks but then less and less and during the last two weeks we had only some flour which mama had saved. She mixed it with water, made some buns the size of my palms, and baked them on the top of the little iron stove. Fortunately, there was some wood piled up in the pantry so at least we were warm. Mama would not take one bite from those buns. It was useless to plead with her. She said "I want you and the child to live for your husband. What will I tell him when he gets back and asks if I took good care of you?" Your mother was wonderful to us. I will never forget it.

On Christmas night an air-raid started which was heavier than ever before. At first everybody thought they had started to kill us with machine guns. There were rumours that they wanted to exterminate the people of the ghetto. but it wasn't that. The attacks lasted three or four days and nights. Huge bombs fell all over the city. When a big one fell just a few inches in front of the house, we got permission to move to the ground floor because of the small children. We got a very small room and thirteen of us moved in, including five children.

One day a man opened the door and stepped in. Guess what, my dear! It was your father who had escaped from Austria and who had been taken to the ghetto by a policeman. He went door-to-door asking about us. Now we were all together, except you. A few days later our dear friend Tony, Andy's godfather, came in. I was so happy to see him and when he gave a piece of bread to Andy I almost kissed his hand. The poor child was so hungry he begged for bread, he would show with his tiny fingers just how small a piece of bread he wanted. But we had none. I was awfully hungry too, and was often half asleep from hunger. In front of my eyes I always saw food. But I didn't care for myself. I only wanted Andy to get some food. When Tony saw us suffering from hunger, he promised that he would bring some bread no matter what. There was already block-to-block fighting in the city between Germans and Russians and no civilians were permitted to go out on the streets.

We were a couple of days away from freedom Tony told us. He comforted us and promised that in two days we were going to be free. He went out for the promised bread, and never came back. Later I learned that a German soldier had killed him. I feel awful that he died because of me, because he wanted to bring food for us when he was not supposed to leave the house.

The next day Thursday, the 18th of January 1945, I saw the first Russian soldier in the yard. We were unimaginably happy! We were allowed to go home, but papa couldn't. He was lying on the couch unconscious. I ran home as fast as my weak body could tolerate but our apartment was a mess. It had been occupied first by German soldiers, who had fled when the Russians came, and then the Russians had taken their place. I went to our superintendent and asked for some food. She gave me some bread, coffee, sugar, jam and a small bottle of milk. I ran back out, out of breath. I was very weak, but the joy of our freedom gave me strength. Besides, I was afraid papa would die before he got any nourishment. Mama made coffee and papa, who came to life with the aid of a doctor, drank some of it. Then mama fixed some lunch which was heavenly! It was coffee with milk and sugar and bread with jam. After I gave a piece of bread with jam on top of it to Andy he was so happy that he was laughing, crying, and jumping with joy all at the same time.

After lunch we all went home. It seemed that we had just escaped from the throat of death. But our dear friend Tony hadn't lived to see this moment. And neither had many millions of Jews who had died from hunger, were shot to death, or thrown into the icy water of the Danube, wounded first by guns. And then there were those who were killed in the gas chambers. We suffered so much, but I know others suffered more. Much, much more!

The fate of my dear parents and two of my sisters and their family, I learned from a newspaper. The Jewish population of Pécs and its outskirts were taken away on 4 July 1944. The article described how they were crowded into cattle wagons seventy to eighty people in one car and sealed without any food or drink. By the time they arrived at Auschwitz after days of travelling many of the people were already dead. In Auschwitz they were sorted out and children and old people and also pregnant women were put into gaschambers and then cremated.

After I read the article I was sick to my stomach. Merciful God! Where were you? How did you let it happen? My poor old parents! They never hurt anybody. They were quiet and diligent; hard working people. They had just started to have a bit easier life after all of us got married.

While we were in the ghetto I had a strong feeling that we would pull through that horrible time. I wanted to live for you! I want you back! You will come back, won't you dearest? I am waiting for you with all my heart and all my love!

Your loving wife, Ibi.

As I wrote in the letter, I felt strongly that Zolti would come home and that he was alive. And at that time he was still alive. Very, very sick but alive. However, I learned much later, that on 18 February 1945 he was shot to death by Germans. He would have been 31 years old in March.

While I was in the ghetto I never heard the name of Raoul Wallenberg. Not even after we were liberated did I hear his name. It took a few years to learn who this man was and that I and many thousands of Hungarian Jews owed our lives to him. He was a Swedish diplomat whose name is almost a legend today, known not only by Hungarian Jews but by people all over the world. He was 32 when he accepted an offer to go to Hungary as the Swedish Humanitarian attache to the Swedish Consul in Budapest.

Wallenberg was a dedicated lover of freedom. He arrived in Budapest on 6 July 1944. First, he helped and saved only Swedish citizens. But later on he helped groups in danger whether they were Swedish or not. He was notified of the gathering of Jews in the racetrack on 16 October 1944. Because of his intervention we were freed. Also, two days before the ghetto was liberated by the Russians, Wallenberg learned from reliable sources of a plan to wipe out the ghetto by mines or machine guns. On 16 January 1945 Wallenberg was notified that in the Royal Hotel some 500 German soldiers and 22 Arrow Cross members had gathered, and that they wanted 200 Hungarian police to participate in the killing. They wanted to start the same night. Wallenberg, fearing for his life in the last days before liberation, was in hiding. But one of his men, on Wallenberg's advice, asked for an audience with Schmidthuber, a German General who was responsible for organizing the killing. The man warned the General that Wallenberg would see to it that he would be tried as a murderer if he didn't stop this crime. That was an effective measure and the General instructed all the people involved to stop the killing.

I did not know that for 48 hours the people of the ghetto were in the hands of God and that only a miracle could have saved us. That miracle had happened thanks to Wallenberg.

After the war

In April and May of 1945, when the survivors started to come home, I went to the railroad station every day. I met some of Zolti's comrades and with thumping heartbeat and much hope I asked about him. No one seemed to know anything about my husband. Finally, one comrade gave me a name and address saying that this man had a list of those who had survived. Happily I ran home and told my in-laws that I was going to that address immediately. I remember on my way there I bought some candy for my son. All the way I was very hopeful and happy. Only when I reached the house did it hit me. I felt an awful sensation. When the man asked my relationship to Zolti, I told him that I was his sister. Then he told me what had happened to him. I cried out, "No! It is not true! My husband promised me he would come home!" The comrade became very angry that I had not told him the truth about my relationship to Zolti. On my way home I stuffed my handkerchief into my mouth so as not to cry out loud.

I didn't have to say anything to my in-laws. Seeing me, they knew what had happened. But they didn't believe it either. They took Andy and went to the address to talk to the man. They thought that he was mistaken and that he had given me the wrong information. Unfortunately it was true. The man told my in-laws that Zolti had had typhus. He also told them that there was a comrade of his who did everything to save Zolti's life, but he couldn't. This comrade's name was Bela Boros. The man also told my in-laws what he hadn't told me, that the Germans shot Zolti dead on 18 February 1945 because of his illness. Mama and papa didn't tell me about the shooting for a long time.

How I managed to live without my darling I don't know. On the street when I saw a tall young man coming towards me I didn't look at his face and pretended that he was Zolti. I pretended that he would hug me like he had a long time ago. I played this game for a long time. Finally I had to face the truth. Zolti, my darling, my beloved husband, was gone and I had to accept the loss.

It was also in April 1945 when my sister, Elizabeth, walked through the door of our building. I didn't recognize her. Her hair was gone because of typhus and she seemed not more than forty kilogrammes. After our emotional meeting the first thing I did was put her into bed and feed her bit by bit every two hours. After a long period of time when she was strong enough to talk I asked her to tell me her story.

On the 11 November 1944 police took her from Aranka's bungalow. By that time Aranka and her daughter were hiding with false papers. Elizabeth was taken to a sports field. From there, with thousands and thousands of other women, she had to walk to a brick factory. They arrived by night and the next morning, for work, they walked to a village which was still in Hungary. Their job was to dig ramparts miles and miles long. They were there for about three weeks. They were women aged sixteen to forty. Every morning they had to get up at 4:30 in the morning. After they drank a cup of weak, black coffee they started their half-hour walk carrying their spades and hoes. Their lunch was some soup and a small piece of bread. When there was an air-raid they stopped working, knelt down in the rampart, and prayed for a fast death by a bomb.

After about three weeks they had to march to the Hungarian-Austrian border where the Germans took them over. By that time many of them had died. They again were placed in a huge empty factory in Lichtenworth, Austria. The life in that concentration camp was unimaginable. They lay on rotten straw like sardines. There nobody had to work. The German plan was to starve all three thousand women to death. It was almost successful. Only a few hundred survived. Elizabeth also got typhus in the last few weeks. On 1 April 1945 the Russian Army liberated the camps. Those who had enough strength started to walk home. Elizabeth was too sick and weak to walk. She and many others stayed behind for some time. People opened the food storage cellar and took what they could. There was some sugar, jam and honey. Elizabeth went on her hands and knees and if a woman had not pitied her she would have received nothing. She was given some sugar cubes and water. The Russian soldiers killed some cows and left them for the starving people. They built a fire and there were fights over the raw meat. Again somebody gave my sister some of it when it was cooked.

After a few days, with two other women, my sister too started her journey home. They walked from Lichtenworth to Gyor in Hungary. They walked two weeks. On their way village people gave them food and shelter for the night in their barns. In one of the villages they found an empty house; the occupants had fled from the Russians. Four other women were there already. They occupied the beds and Elizabeth and her two companions lay on the floor. Somehow my sister had saved her good winter coat and she put it on for cover. The blanket she had given to the other two. Suddenly, she was awakened by a flashlight. A Russian soldier stood above her saying, "Burzsuj," because he had seen her good coat. He pulled Elizabeth up by her hand but she fell back when he released her. He asked in German, "What is wrong with you? Are you sick?" And then Elizabeth saved herself from a probable rape with the one word which came to her mind.

She said, "Syphilis." The Russian jumped back and the rest of the women were also saved. The soldiers even gave them bread and a couple of rabbits which they had killed and which the women baked and ate. The next day they continued their journey and this time they all managed to get on a train to Budapest. Elizabeth stayed with us for a couple of weeks and with careful nursing and a doctor's care she slowly got her strength back. Then she went to Aranka's to stay for another few weeks. When she was strong enough, Elizabeth took a train to our home town, Pécs, to see if anyone from her husband's family was alive. She found only a sister-in-law. Elizabeth's husband, his seventeen-year-old brother, and their parents perished in Auschwitz.

Elizabeth stayed in Pécs with her sister-in-law for a year. She was introduced to a man who had also lost his wife and two sons in the Holocaust. They were married in 1946. Their only child, a son Tomi, was born in 1948. They moved to Budapest the following year and my sister's husband, Frank, worked as a cutter in a cloth factory.

My other sister, Aranka, had a different story. Her husband was also in a concentration camp. Aranka managed to get false papers for herself and Marianna. There was an organization called "Home for girls" run by nuns. This was a home for mostly young women who came up to the capital from smaller cities to work and had no place to stay. They had to pay for their board. Later, the nuns gave shelter to those who were bombed out of their homes. Aranka said she was one of them. There were some Jews in hiding amongst the refugees. The Mother Superior knew about them but she didn't know that my sister and her daughter were also Jews. There were strict rules. No boys were allowed to visit the girls. By nine o'clock at night everyone had to be home. The food was sparse with little variety.

One day the head nun approached my sister and told her that they both had to confess to the priest. "I just did it last month," Aranka said.

"Then your little girl must do it," replied the nun.

"Mommy, what can I say to the priest? What is a confess anyway?" Aranka's daughter asked her when she was told about the confession.

"Just be calm darling and lie a little bit, saying that you stole an apple or didn't tell the truth about something," answered her mother.

"What will the priest say after I confess those things?" she wanted to know.

"He will say that he forgives you for your sins and that is all." Marianna did what she was told. When she came out from the chapel she was so relieved that she started to laugh and with dancing steps she went to her mother.

The Mother Superior saw it and she said angrily, "Aren't you ashamed of yourself? You just confessed and already you are laughing and dancing?" The poor child didn't know that she was not supposed to do these things after the confession.

The priest must have known that the girl was Jewish. On Christmas day he gave a beautiful sermon. In it he said, "Don't mind the enemies today. Love and humanity will keep us all together." Aranka and her daughter managed to stay there until the city was freed from the Germans but there were awful moments when the Arrow Cross bandits or Germans went in to look for hiding Jews. There were about sixty of them. Because every one of them had false papers, and the Mother Superior knew about most of them and defended them, they were left alone.

Aranka's husband, Jeno, escaped to the Russians at the end and he came to Budapest with them when they liberated us on 18 January 1945.

Margaret's husband, Vilmos, died in the early 1940s. He was buried in Pécs and Margaret came to the cemetery from her village quite often to visit the grave. One day, as she was sitting on a bench at the front of the tombstone, a man came over and politely asked her if he could sit down. They started to talk and the man told Margaret that he had lost his wife not long ago and that her tombstone was beside Margaret's husband's. They talked about their spouses' illnesses and their deaths. The man, Joseph Halmos, was a gentile but his wife had been Jewish as was his teenage son. Margaret and Joseph became friends and soon they fell in love. After a time, Joseph proposed to Margaret and she happily accepted. Unfortunately, there were already restrictive laws for Jews and Joseph as a gentile as not allowed to marry a Jewess. On his advice Margaret gave up her store and home and moved in with him. Joe also had a grocery store in the outskirts of the city and an apartment behind the store. That period of time while they were together was the happiest time in Margaret's life. Unfortunately, this happiness was short-lived.

When the Jewish population was rounded up for the ghetto Joseph couldn't do anything for Margaret. He jumped on his bicycle and escorted them for a distance, as far as he could. Then hiding his tear-soaked face from the gendarmes he watched as the Jews were herded into the ghetto. Joseph's son, Tomi, who was only 18 years old, had been taken away earlier to a forced labour camp. He never returned.

In 1946 I went to Pécs with my son to see what had happened to father's shop. Joseph invited us to stay in his home.

To my regret my father's shop was burned out. When and how it happened I didn't know. My son and I stayed a few weeks there because the fresh country air was good for the child. Besides, Andy liked Joe very much. They became good friends and Joe also loved my son. Joseph still talked about Margaret a lot and he told me that when Margaret mentioned to mother that she wanted to move in with him mother was very much against it. But because of the circumstances mother reconsidered and she even made a nice fish supper for their engagement.

Before I left for Budapest Joe said to me, "Neither of us can live with the dead, my dear. Would you consider marrying me?" It came to me as a big surprise and in the first minute I didn't know what to say.

Then I gathered my thoughts and replied, "Sorry, Joseph, but first of all the age difference is too much between us. Secondly, I couldn't live here ever again. The memories of everything about the city are just too much for me. And also I would feel uncomfortable marrying you when I know how much you and my sister loved each other and how happy she was with you." He accepted my refusal and understood me. I was 29 years old and Joe was 48. Still, when he came to visit us the next summer in Budapest, he told my in-laws how sorry he was that I had refused his proposal.

A year after I wrote that letter to my husband who had never received it I attached another few lines to it. Those few lines I wrote to my little son. I still treasure both of those original letters written in Hungarian, together with some of Zolti's postcards from concentration camp.

Budapest, 10 February 1946

My dear little son, Andy.

You are a small boy yet, only three and a half years old. You were with us in that terrible time but you didn't know what was happening. You did not know why you couldn't get a bite of bread when you were awfully hungry, and you don't know why you had no father. I wrote a letter to your daddy to tell him what had happened to us. I felt very strongly that he must come back to us. Since then I have found out he will never come back because he was sick and the Germans shot him to death 18 February 1945, one year ago today. I still cry for him with painful tears and I will cry until I am dead.

Now I will keep this letter for you because I want you to know what happened to us when you are old enough to understand. Be my good little boy always. God help me to raise you.

Your loving mother.

My work in a children's home

I began to arrange my life without my husband. I started to work in a dressmaker's shop. We were all young women there and two were wives of Zolti's comrades. We became friends. I stayed with my in-laws, who actually wouldn't have let me go even if I could, and mama took care of Andy.

One day a comrade of Zolti's came to visit me. His pregnant wife had been killed in Auschwitz. They had lived in the outskirts of Budapest and the young pregnant woman was taken away before she had time to escape to the city where she had an aunt.

The man, Bela Boros, was very alone. He had nobody left in his family. He was short and not very good looking. His bushy and slightly curly hair needed a cut most of the time. In his narrow face his lower lip was thicker than the upper one. But his eyes were huge and blue like the water of our Lake Balaton and they showed concern and understanding for people. After his first visit he asked me if he could come to see us more often. Andy and Bela loved each other from the beginning. I told Bela I didn't want a boyfriend and I added that maybe I never would. He said he just wanted to be with us as a friend. In this I agreed and most of the time we took Andy with us. They were such good company for each other. I remember an outing to an *espresso* bar, the name we gave to little coffeehouses where we could sit and talk with a cup of coffee and piece of cake for hours.

We took Andy with us. He wanted to go to the washroom so I showed him where it was. When he came out he said, "Mommy, the washroom is very beautiful. I have to go again." So he went. After he came out he asked me loudly, "Mommy, don't you have to go to make pipi?" He was four years old. He wanted very much for me to see the beautiful washroom.

Many times we went on excursions and when Andy got tired Bela would carry him on his back. Bela spent more and more time with us and he said that he was in love with me. In the summer of 1947 when Bela asked me to marry I told him to give me a few days to think it over. I asked my in-laws for their opinion. They didn't oppose it because they knew how much Bela liked their grandson. After a few days I told Bela I would marry him. He bought a gold wedding band and we were engaged.

Bela and I met almost daily. I recall a cute episode with my son. One day the two of us took a long bus ride. Andy, being a friendly little boy, became involved in a discussion with a woman on the bus. I heard Andy mention Bela's name a few times. Finally the woman asked him, "Who is uncle Bela?" My son was silent for a few seconds not knowing how to describe his uncle Bela. Then he said, "He is the man who takes my mother out every night."

Bela inherited his aunt's apartment and we planned to move there after marriage. Our friendship was one-sided because I had no special emotional attachment to him. I accepted his proposal because I felt lonely and also because I was sure he would be a good father for Andy.

Bela very seldom talked about his wife and unborn child. All I know is that she was a teacher and, coincidentally, she had the same first name as mine. However, I talked a lot about Zolti and Bela was patient and understanding. He started to talk about leaving the country. That was the reason that he was not in a hurry to get married. His plan was to escape alone to Vienna and then he would send for us and together we would go to Israel. I saw that he was afraid to take the responsibility of taking us with him.

During our courtship I changed my job and went to work at an orphanage for Jewish children. I had always wanted to work with children. The orphanage was sponsored by the American Jewish Congress and was called "Louise Wise's Home for Children." It was far away from the city and I had to live in. Andy stayed with his grandparents and went to a nearby kindergarten. The home was comprised of two buildings at the edge of the forest of Buda. The main centre was in the middle of about eighteen acres of a park which the children enjoyed. The smaller house was for certain staff members who were required to live on the grounds.

Some mornings I got up earlier to have a walk on the rolling hills, marvelling at the huge pine trees and lovely flower beds, watching the sun rise and listening to the songs of different birds. During winter we could toboggan down the hills which I enjoyed as much as the children.

At the time of my arrival at the orphanage the children had never been allowed to go outside the building. That was the doctor's orders. I didn't know the reason, I just thought maybe he was afraid that the children would get some disease if they contacted the outside world. I started to hint to the authorities that they should let the kids out of the home. I didn't think it was healthy to completely isolate them even though they had everything they needed in the home. The children were between the ages of three and nine years. They all had only either one parent or a grandparent or an aunt or only a distant relative. Some had nobody at all.

I had to take care of a group of girls between four and eight years old. I loved my girls. They knew my feelings and the children asked for love with every hug and touch they gave me. My work with them was more than a job and a much-needed salary. It gave me pleasure while I performed good deeds. I took care of the children's physical needs and occupied the little ones while the older girls attended school in the building school room. Every second Sunday there were visiting hours. This meant big excitement for the children. Unfortunately there were some who had no visitors so we spent extra time with them. We had roughly fifty or sixty children divided into different groups. There were five governesses, one teacher, cleaning staff and a cook.

Before the visiting day I would bathe my girls and wash their hair. In the morning I would give each of them a white pinafore to wear over their dresses and white ribbons for their hair. I would braid their hair in pigtails since most had long hair. All clean and beautiful and with shining eyes they would then gather at the gate and wait for their visitors. I was happy when I received compliments on the children's appearance and was thanked for the good care and love I gave them.

I had only one day off a week to be at home. Usually I left for my break in the evening after I had put my girls to bed. After I tucked them in and kissed them good night they would remind me not to forget to return with a treat for them and I always did. Bela would wait for me at the bus station and we went to a movie or just spent a quiet evening at his apartment listening to his opera records. Around eleven o'clock he would escort me home. By that time my in-laws and Andy were in bed. Andy would have been in bed already even if I had gone straight home from the orphanage so by delaying my return I could spend some time with my fiance. Arriving home I would tip-toe to my son's bed, kiss the sleeping child gently and then go to my own bed. The following day was spent entirely with my son. On some Sundays he would come to visit me with his grandparents in the children's home.

One day I received good news from the principal of the orphanage. Finally the doctor in charge of the children had given permission for them to go outdoors. "Children! Children!" I called, clapping my hands on a sunny Sunday morning, "I have big news for you! Guess what? We have received permission from Miss Eva to go for a picnic in the forest. After breakfast you should go to your room to change out of your good shoes because outside it is still muddy from the early morning rain. Also, don't forget to bring a sweater. Then all of you must go to the gate and wait for me." I still remember the excitement of the twelve little girls after my announcement. While they went to their room to change I went to the kitchen to ask the cook to make packages of sandwiches and fruit for the children

I took the picnic basket from the kitchen and went to meet the girls. I unlocked the gate and for the first time we happily marched out. The children were laughing, chatting, and singing as we walked. We didn't have to walk far to reach the forest which was called Buda Mountain. It was full of huge pine trees and wild flowers in the colours of blue, yellow, white and lilac. The smells and sounds of the early summer hit me and I inhaled them deeply. We walked for some time and when we came to a small glade we stopped and I spread out a blanket. The girls played games and picked flowers. They were so excited when they saw a rabbit, a squirrel or a deer. Soon they got hungry and we sat down to eat our lunch which tasted so good. After lunch the girls picked some more wild flowers and each carried a bouquet home to present to Miss Eva, the director of the home. After that, our first outing, they even let us go the city by the mountain train.

After doing my job for about a year I could no longer stand to be apart from my son. Because the management was afraid I would leave my work they allowed Andy, who was now five years old, to come and live at the orphanage. He was put in a different group and instead of calling me "mother" he had to address me by my first name. I understood and went along with this demand.

While the school-age children were in class I tended to the younger ones. On one occasion I taught them to perform a play about the characters of Purim. I was more excited and nervous then they were before the performance. However, the play went smoothly in front of an audience though only I understood some of the speeches by the younger children.

Of all my girls I remember Agnes best. We called her "Agi" for short. She was seven years old, with shiny black hair, big brown eyes and a narrow, classic face with just a touch of freckles. Agi limped slightly and very seldom smiled. Those beautiful brown eyes were sad most of the time. She wanted to be loved very much. Her parents had been killed in the Holocaust. Agi had only a grandmother and a retarded aunt who lived with the grandmother.

My sister, Aranka, and her husband had only one child, their daughter, Marianna. They couldn't have any more children and they wanted to adopt one. When I mentioned the children in the orphanage they decided to come over to see them. From the first moment they saw Agi they liked her. After they got permission they took her home a few weeks for the weekend. Agi was happy and liked her parents- and sister-to-be so very much that she asked if she could call them "mother" and "father." Agi's grandmother agreed to the adoption. The child had already lived with my sister and her family for about three months. She went to school and was prepared to be with her adopted family. Marianna was thirteen or fourteen years old at that time and she too liked her little sister-to-be.

One day Agi's grandmother came over to take her granddaughter home for a visit. Only Marianna was at home at the time. The grandmother asked that a special dress be put on Agi. Marianna refused the request saying that the dress had to be saved for school the next day. The grandmother got very angry and took the child and all her belongings back to the orphanage. When Marianna's parents got home and learned what had happened they went to get the girl back. However, the old lady seemed to have completely changed her mind about the adoption. Agi was heartbroken. Aranka took her to their home a few more times to visit but when the time came to return to the orphanage Agi was sadder and more withdrawn then ever. How unfortunate it was to deprive the child of a loving family because of the spite of an old woman.

Some years later Marianna saw a little girl on the street who was very much like Agi. She also limped a little. The girl could not have been Agi because she would have been grown up but still Marianna went home almost crying, remembering the child who had almost become her sister.

When Andy grew to school age I left my job in the orphanage and got another job in a kindergarten in the city so I could go home daily. The kindergarten was private and parents had to pay for their children's care. This was quite different from the orphanage. The only similarity was that I still worked with children. Most of them were well-to-do and spoiled. There were about twenty-five children aged between three and six. We had to occupy them with all manner of things like painting, drawing, games and reading story books. They were there from nine in the morning until four or five in the afternoon. They ate their lunch there which was cooked by a woman in a kitchen separated from the classroom. In the mid-morning we took them out to the nearby park for a couple of hours. After lunch they had to lie down on little cots spread on the floor in the big, sunny classroom.

Andy went to a nearby elementary school and his teachers liked him very much. Despite the awful things he had been through he was a very lovable and kind child. He resembled his father with the same wide forehead and narrowing face. Only, unlike his father, Andy's eyes were of a green tint and his hair was lighter in colour and straight. I always dressed him nicely and he never had to be ashamed of his looks. Because his daddy had been a sportsman he also wanted his son to be one. Therefor, Andy was taught many sports. By the tender age of five he was already able to swim, to skate and to ride a bicycle. He loved swimming best and he still does.

Papa, who worked in one of the spas, had to join a political party. There were two parties, the Communists and the Socialists. Papa became a Communist. He attended seminars and later gave lectures. Living with my in-laws I felt that I wasn't grown up yet. They helped us in every way they could but they would never let me go on my own. I wished for even one single room somewhere separate from them where I could be on my own and which I could share with my son. I would never have that wish come true as long as I stayed in Hungary. When I applied for an apartment of my own I was told by the authorities that I had a roof over my head and I should be happy with it.

In the first years after the war if any man came to visit me and sat on the divan, mama got upset. She said that nobody should sit on that couch which belonged to and was used by her son.

After those men who had been taken away and who had survived came back and discovered that their families were wiped out they all wanted to marry and to start a new family. I was asked by a few in the first year after the war ended, but I wasn't ready to marry yet.

However, there was one young man, Paul, who came to visit my in-laws. He had been a friend of Zolti's in their home-town and he was tall and handsome and somehow reminded me of my darling husband. Eventually he confessed that he visited us to ask me to marry him so I asked him, "Why do you want to marry a widow with a child when you could choose among many single girls?"

"Because I was a friend of your husband and I always liked you and I know that you had a good marriage," he answered. He also wanted to go to the United States or Australia and to take Andy and myself with him. When I mentioned to mama that maybe it would be a good idea to leave every bad thing behind and to start a new life far away from home, mama again was upset and cried.

"I know this man," she said. "He is a penny-pincher and wouldn't give the child what he needs." So as long as I lived with them I had no chance to live my own life. It is not that I didn't like them and was very grateful. I was very grateful but still, it was not the same as when my husband had lived with us. The only man they liked was Bela. Bela had been Zolti's best comrade and had tried to save him in the camp. I remember that Zolti wrote about Bela and wrote about how nice and good-hearted he was and he even mentioned that if anything happened to him, Bela would take care of Andy and me. He jokingly called him "bust statue" because of his height.

It was the summer of 1948 when Bela had the opportunity to escape. He promised me that he would send for us as soon as he was able. But it was many months until a peasant woman knocked on our door. She gave me a note from Bela and in the note he set a date for us to accompany that woman. Fortu-nately, papa was not home when the woman came. I told the plan to mama and somehow she didn't object. Maybe because she knew how much Bela liked her grandson. But we had to keep it from papa because being a communist at that time he would never have agreed to let us go.

First escape and jail

One bright and mild October day Andy and I went to a railway station where I would meet the woman and another couple who also wanted to escape. Mama wanted to escort us to the station. I was afraid that she would cry but she promised she wouldn't. How hard it had been for her, knowing our intentions and not being able to show her feelings! But she was strong. Mama even got on the train and came with us for a short while. Then she kissed us, wished us luck, and got off the train at the first stop. The other couple and the peasant woman were sitting in different rows. I had to watch the woman to know where to get off. It was a village near the Czechoslovakian border where she got off and we followed her. We went to her home where we had to wait until dark.

I thought it was time to explain the situation to my son. As I mentioned earlier, Andy adored my fiance, so I told him we were going to another country to meet uncle Bela, who would become his new daddy. However, we had to be very quiet and careful because there were border guards and if they captured us they would put us in jail. Andy, who was seven years old, understood my explanation and was very co-operative.

After dark we started our journey. Often we had to walk uphill which was very tiring. After a couple of hours Andy whispered, "Mommy, I'm very tired. Let's take a rest now."

"Please, darling, don't sit down," I replied. "If you sit down we will get lost because we will lose the others." My son wanted to be brave and he walked some more. But after another hour he couldn't go any further. I went up to the woman and said that Andy couldn't keep up. The woman carried him on her back and he fell asleep in a minute. I was also very tired and the knapsack on my back was getting heavier by the moment. I thought, as I walked, how nice it would be to leave this heavy burden behind! No, I can't do that, I thought because everything we own is in the knapsack. Not that it was much, only a change of clothes for both of us, an extra pair of shoes, some toilet articles and two towels. Not even a toy for my son. As we walked, I said a silent prayer. "Dear God, please let us reach the border safely, let us start a new life in a free country. I don't have to tell you how much we suffered from our fellow Hungarians, how they hunted us like animals. You saved my son's life when he was a very sick baby in the ghetto and I'm thankful for it even if you let my young husband be killed. Please, save us again, my God." But this time my prayer went unanswered.

Suddenly I saw a bright flash in the dark and a voice yelled "Stop or I will shoot!" We were caught by the Czechoslovakian border guards.

We were so close, so very close to freedom! The woman, with Andy on her back, disappeared behind a hill. The rest of us stopped. Then, not seeing my son I ran after them screaming, "Stop! Stop! Bring my child back!" Finally, the woman stopped and came back to us.

The border guards escorted us to their barracks. Much later I was informed that there was an arrangement between the border guards and the peasant woman to capture everyone she took to the border. She was a traitor. We were very tired by the time we arrived at the barracks. There they searched us and took all my money and valuables. There wasn't much but it was everything that I had. I had hidden the money in a variety of places under the cover of a chocolate bar and behind the lining of my purse. They found it all except two one-hundred forint bills. What happened to those bills I will explain later. In the barracks office we lay down on a cot. One guard offered his own cot for Andy and me. The others lay on the floor. Andy slept through the night but I stayed awake wondering, as so often in the past, what the morning would bring.

The next day two guards took us back to the Hungarian border on foot. The Hungarians locked us in their military station where we were put in the detention centre. Andy and I were in one room and the others were in another. For a few days nothing happened. We got the same food as the soldiers and one straw mattress on which we both slept. They allowed us out into the building's yard for one hour every day. I begged the guard to let the boy stay out a bit longer. When our time was up my poor child never wanted to go back to the cell. To request privileges was useless. The guard would not let my son stay any longer than was permitted.

One day when we returned from the walk Andy ran back to the yard and picked up two small stones. Later he whispered in my ear that the next time we returned to our cell he would put the two stones under the door and therefor it could not be locked. My heart was aching for my little son.

The only pastime which Andy had was to cut paper airplanes with my manicure scissors. When the guard through the peephole saw the activity he came in and demanded the scissors from the boy. I don't know how it happened but the small scissors disappeared in front of our eyes. When Andy refused to give them to the guard he got really angry and threatened to spank the child. Finally I asked my son to give them to me. "Okay," he said, "but uncle guard has to turn his back to me." The guard was co-operative and Andy pulled the scissors from under his shirt. Now the only thing Andy played with was gone. "What can I do all day, Mommy?" he asked me.

The cell had a very small window close to the ceiling. We carried the mattress to a place under the window and leaned it lengthwise against the wall. Then we climbed up and sat on the window sill to look out at the street. The military barrack was on the outskirts of the city so the street was not a busy one. There were sidewalks on both sides of the street and alongside of the sidewalk were *akacz* trees, the native trees of Hungary. We were not able to see many passersby but still we were a bit occupied just looking out and counting the few cars and pedestrians. I had written a note and waited for the right moment when somebody would notice us so that I could throw it down to them. In the note I asked that whoever got it go to the Jewish Congregation and to ask them to notify my in-laws in Budapest to come for their grandson. Finally a young man, pushing his bicycle, noticed my frantic waving of the piece of paper. He stopped and bent down pretending to fix his bicycle. Then he looked up and signalled. I threw the note. He picked it up, jumped on his bike and left.

Another two days passed. We were at the window again when I saw a woman approaching on the opposite side of the street. She looked very familiar. Andy saw her too. I had no time to finish my sentence, "Look Andy, that woman looks like your ...."

When my son yelled at the top of his voice "Grandmama!" Mama looked up and motioned that we should be silent. Her face showed a sorrow and a sadness which I would never forget. Later she told us that the Jewish Congress had notified them to come immediately for their grandson. My mother-in-law came with a man from the Congress who went in first and told mama to wait outside.

Before they let Andy go home with his grandmother the major of the guards asked the boy to step into the office. I don't know what the conversation was between them. However, later the major told me that had it been within his power he would have set us free. The officer congratulated my son for being such a bright little fellow. Andy was still in the office and mama was also called in for questioning. Earlier I had informed Andy that two hundred forints were sewn into his coat cuffs. My instructions to him were that only when he and grandma were safely out of the building could he tell her about the money. As soon as my mother-in-law stepped into the office, Andy said, "Grandmama, when we are out on the street and alone I will tell you a secret." The major was humane and intelligent enough not to ask the child about his secret.

I felt better that Andy was going home and back to school. I was concerned about my future. I had sinned and was going to be punished for my action. My crime was that I had attempted to leave my country where we had suffered so much. I sinned because all I wanted was a peaceful life for my son and myself.

The next day I was transferred from the military station to the nearest city, Miskolc. It was night again when we arrived at the jail. I was put in a very small cell. There were two women each lying on a narrow cot. After the door was locked behind me I stood there feeling very faint. Right then I remembered a childhood dream. Every night when mother read the newspaper out loud to the family the word "jail" was often mentioned. I had repeated dreams that I was in jail and awakened terrified that jail would be my destiny. Now there I was, my childhood nightmares had become a reality. As I stood in the semi-darkness unable to move or to cry from shock I felt a gentle hand on my shoulders. One of the women led me to her cot with an offer to share it with me. I thanked her for her kindness and comfort and accepted her offer. Weeks later I heard the rumour that she was a murderer.

The next morning I was transferred into a larger cell but it was still far to small for all the prisoners in it. All the women were Jewish dissidents. I don't remember how many beds were pushed together but we lay on them like sardines during the night. When one of us had to turn over the entire row turned otherwise we would not have had enough room. There was only one single bed in a corner in case somebody got sick. In the other corner of the cell there was a pail to be used as a toilet. We managed to hang a bed sheet around it. Also there were a couple of basins which were used for washing ourselves and our laundry. Every day it was required that we go to the yard and to move in circles for one hour. We were forbidden to speak to one another. But the old time prisoners always managed to exchange news or little written notes with each other. I didn't like to go because many times there were disturbances amongst the criminals. One day a woman ran from the circle and jumped on another woman screaming, "You pig, you dirty pig, I'm here because of you! Because you denounced me!" She started to hit the woman and there was a big fist-fight. The guards ran over and took the attacker away. I also recognised the peasant woman who betrayed us and I cursed her in my thoughts but I wouldn't make a scene. I was satisfied when I heard a rumour that she was sentenced for one year in prison. Later, however, it came to my knowledge that it wasn't true. The woman, being an informer, spent only a few days in prison and then she was set free.

It was not expected that we would have to work the way the long-term inmates did. We tried to create a routine for ourselves. Mornings we took one of the grey blankets which we used for cover during the night and spread it on the floor. We stripped off to our panties and bras and did some exercises. A woman amongst us was appointed our gymnastics teacher. All participated with the exception of two elderly women. First we lay on our backs and raised our legs up and down several times. Then we did some sit-ups and push-ups and some of us who knew how did bridges. Lying on our backs we curved them and pulled our legs as close to our arms as we could. We did those exercises for about thirty minutes. We didn't even care that sometimes the male guards were watching us through the peephole. We learned about this activity from a male dissident whose mother was with us. The men's cells were just opposite to us on the same corridor.

We took turns doing our own laundry. The jail had a library so at least we had some books to read. We all had the privilege of getting kosher food from the Jewish Congress. That lunch was the highlight of the day and of course it was much better food than was provided by the jail. Unfortunately the light went off at nine p.m. and so the nights were very long because nobody could fall asleep at that hour. We talked in the dark and made a rule that only one person was allowed to talk at one time on any subject that she chose. We talked about our home, our plans for the future, our escape, how we were caught, about our families and what food we liked. None of us talked about our experiences during the Holocaust. It was still very vivid and very painful.

Two women guards were appointed to watch us. One was a malicious spinster with a bad temper. The other was a married woman who was not so bad.

Soon my trial date arrived. I was convicted and sentenced to six months. For me it was unimaginable that I would stay for that length of time. My lawyer advised me to appeal. He was hired by the Jewish Consulate. They even deposited some money at the lawyer's office to be given to me when I was free.

After my first trial I became ill. I had a constant fever and the doctor couldn't figure out the cause. The jail's doctor sent me with some male prisoners and guards to the city's hospital

Elizabeth, Mother, Aranka, Father, Ibolya (Ibi) Szalai 1921

Ignacz Szalai, W.W.I.

Margaret and Ilona Szalai, 1920

Zionist Youth Group, 1933, Ibi Szalai, second from left

Engagement, 1939, Ibi Szalai and Zoltan (Zolti) Reti

Ignacz and Laura Szalai, 1942

After the Holocaust, 1946

Ibolya and Andras, 1947

*Andras and Ibi, snapshots from
Zoltan Reti's wallet, recovered after
his death in the labour camp.*

The Louise Wise Orphanage, 1948

Andras Reti, 1948

Mother's Day, 1949

Édes jó Anyám!

Édes Anyám szivem minden melegével. köszöntlek ma téged. És megígérem, hogy a nagymamával nem leszek többé goromba.

csókol András.

"For My Dear Mother"

Aranka, Elizabeth and Ibi, 1950

Tomi, Marianna and Andras, 1950

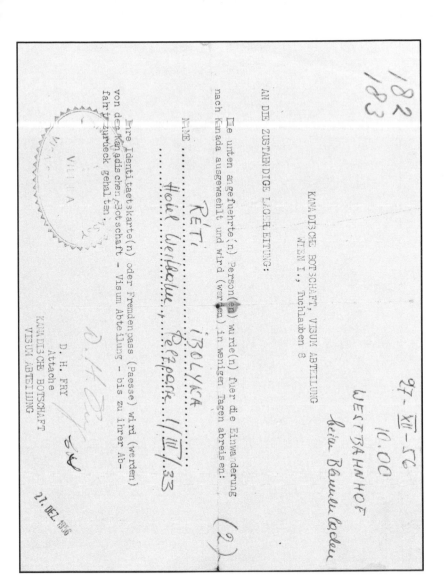

182
183

27 - XII - 56
10.00
WESTBAHNHOF
beim Bummelacker

KANADISCHE BOTSCHAFT, VISUM ABTEILUNG
WIEN I., Tuchlauben 8

AN DIE ZUSTAENDIGE LOGIERLEITUNG:

Die unten angefuehrte(n) Person(en) wurde(n) fuer die Einwanderung
nach Kanada ausgewaehlt und wird (werden) in wenigen Tagen abreisen:

NAME .... RETI   iBOLYKA
Hotel Weilbuche., Belgarie..1/III/.33   (2)

Ihre Identitaetskarte(n) oder Fremdenpass (Paesse) wird (werden)
von der Kanadischen Botschaft - Visum Abteilung - bis zu ihrer Ab-
fahrt zurueck gehalten.

D. H. FRY
Attache
KANADISCHE BOTSCHAFT
VISUM ABTEILUNG

21. DEZ. 1956

Canadian Embassy, Vienna, visa for Canada, 1956

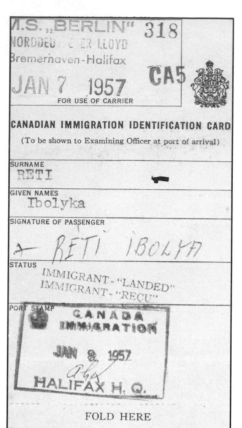

M.S. „BERLIN" 318
NORDDEU___ ER LLOYD
Bremerhaven-Halifax
JAN 7 1957   CA5
FOR USE OF CARRIER

CANADIAN IMMIGRATION IDENTIFICATION CARD

(To be shown to Examining Officer at port of arrival)

SURNAME
RETI

GIVEN NAMES
Ibolyka

SIGNATURE OF PASSENGER
RETI IBOLYA

STATUS
IMMIGRANT - "LANDED"
IMMIGRANT - "REÇU"

PORT STAMP
CANADA
IMMIGRATION
JAN 8 1957
HALIFAX H. Q.

FOLD HERE

DULY STAMPED BY AN IMMIGRATION OFFICER,
THIS CARD IS EVIDENCE OF YOUR STATUS IN
CANADA. IT IS REQUIRED FOR CUSTOMS CLEAR-
ANCE AND WILL ALSO PROVE USEFUL FOR OTHER
PURPOSES.

M.S. Berlin, 1957

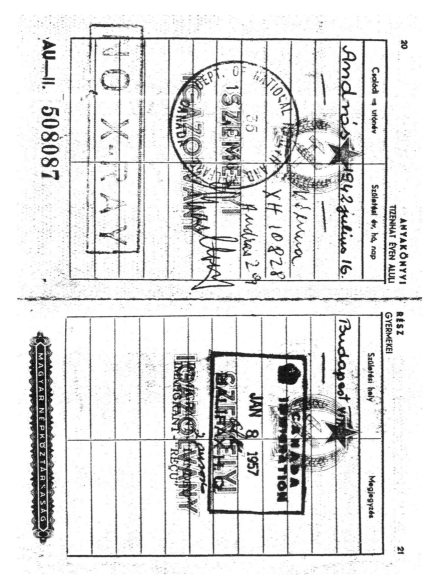

Hungarian Government Identity book, stamped by Canadian
Immigration in lieu of a passport, 1957

In Winnipeg, 1957

In Winnipeg, 1957

Wedding, 1958, Ibi and Emil Grossman

My In-laws, the Reti's, 1958

Together in Canada, Tomi, Elizabeth, Marianna, Aranka, Ibi and Andy, 1960

My In-laws' visit, Toronto, 1963 and their Fiftieth Wedding Anniversary.

Work and retirement

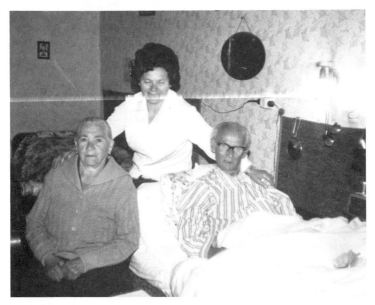

My father-in-law's illness, Budapest, 1972

Andy and his grandmother, Budapest, 1974

Grandchildren, David and Kati, 1982

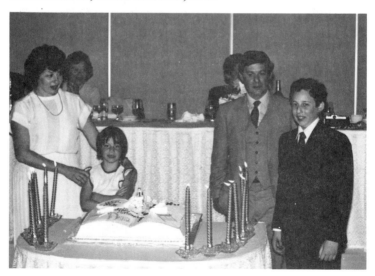

Barmitzvah, 1984, Magdi, Kati, Andy and David

With Andras (David!) in Budapest, 1983

Plaque commemorating the Pécs ghetto, Pécs, Hungary, 1989

"Auschwitz martyrs, **Reine Izraelishe Fat,** *Soap," Pécs, Hungary, 1989*

for an x-ray. Among the men were some dissidents but they were handcuffed the same way as criminals. We walked all the way to the hospital. I was glad that I wasn't handcuffed because even though no one knew me in this strange city I would have felt terribly embarrassed. The x-ray didn't show anything wrong. Back in the jail the doctor gave me a thermometer and instructed me to take my temperature three times a day. The malicious guard was to check it every time. She never did.

Shortly after this my second trial came up. One of my cellmates lent me her coat for this occasion. She was the same height as I but much heavier. The coat was a light brown, good quality camel's hair wool which was soft and warm. It was big enough to wrap around me. The purpose of her lending me the large coat was to show how much weight I had lost.

The judge must have known about my illness because he asked me if it was true that I had a steady temperature. "Yes, your honour, I still have a higher than normal temperature," I replied. Then he asked the guard if she had checked as ordered. The guard didn't expect the question. For a second there was a strained silence. I knew that she had to say yes or it would appear that I had made up the entire story. Worse, the guard knew that she hadn't done her duty.

Finally she said, "Yes, I checked it daily and she has had a fever for weeks." Probably this was the reason that my sentence was reduced to three months.

More than half of my sentence was already over and I was counting the days to my release. The woman guard started to crochet a huge table cover and she gave it to us to work on. We all participated because the time went faster by doing it. Due to my illness I was allowed to occupy a single bed. But in that bed were more bed-bugs than in the others because they came to life with the smell of human flesh which they had missed for a while. Those dreadful bugs could be dried out completely even for years but come alive as soon as they smelled a human presence. I was their victim. I couldn't do anything against their horrible bites which made big blisters all over my body.

I had craved sweets but in the jail there weren't any. On one occasion a girlfriend of mine whose husband had been a comrade of Zolti's sent a beautiful parcel of sweets for me. The guard came in, showed me the contents of the parcel and took it away without giving me even a bite. She said that they would give it to the younger prisoners. It wasn't true! We had a young girl among us also and she didn't receive any of it either. The parcel contained chocolate, candies, cookies, and home-made pastries. It was a kind of pastry which the Hungarians baked around Christmas time. One loaf was filled with poppy-seed and the other with walnuts and raisins. I almost cried when the guard took the parcel away.

Of course, I thought constantly about my little son, Andy, who was seven at that time. I recalled how brave he had been during our attempted escape and also in the detention centre. Every day I imagined my reunion with Andy. I wondered about what he was doing. Was he with his friends or had grandpa taken him to skate? Was he missing me? I hoped that he wasn't sick. I knew that he was in the best of hands with his grandparents but I still missed him very much.

Out of jail

The time for which I had been impatiently waiting arrived at last. I even got out a few days early because it was 21 December 1950, Stalin's birthday. Since Hungary was under Russian occupation they celebrated the "great" leader's birthday by releasing political prisoners on that day.

I hugged my cellmates and warmly thanked a sixteen-year-old girl who had done my laundry while I was sick. I went to the office to receive the documentation for my release and then a guard escorted me to the gate and had another guard open it for me. I stepped out and for a few seconds I stood by the gate of the jail and inhaled the crisp air of winter. How beautiful it was to be free again! I wanted to cry out to the passing people "I am free! I am free! I can go home to my little boy!"

First I went to my lawyer's office where I received my money and from there I went to find a grocery store where I bought a quarter kilogram of white bread and a big bar of chocolate. I ate them on the street; one bite from the bread, one bite from chocolate. I went to the train station to make inquires about the train leaving for Budapest. I bought a ticket for the express train which stopped only two or three times instead of at every village. I had to wait a couple of hours for this train so I bought a newspaper to kill the time. It was full with news of the celebrations for Stalin's birthday.

Finally I heard the train's whistle and when it arrived it stopped just long enough for me to get on. Leaving the station the train went faster and faster and the click-clack of the wheels sounded "I go home. I go home." In about two and one half hours I arrived at the Keleti railway station in Budapest. It was only a twenty-minute walk from my home. I hurried all the way on familiar streets and took a short cut by walking through the park where Andy played with his little friends every day. I walked into our apartment building through the short half-dark corridor to the yard. A few more steps and I stopped at our kitchen door which was the entrance to our apartment. With pounding heart I pushed down on the door-handle and opened the door which usually wasn't locked. I stepped in and there was my son with his grandma eating their supper at the table.

They looked up and my son was so fast jumping off the chair, crying out, "Mommy! Mommy! You are home!" I bent down and as we hugged he squeezed my neck so hard that he almost choked me. I held him and felt that he was the only person in the whole world who belonged to me. At that moment I remembered my Zolti's words. He had said to me, when I cried learning that I was pregnant at that terrible time, "Don't cry, darling. We need this baby, you will see." Andy looked a little bit taller and his big green-gray eyes were shiny with happiness. His soft, light-brown hair was parted at the side and fell onto his forehead as usual and as I watched he brushed it back with one of his hands. He was neatly dressed and clean as he always had been.

Mama waited patiently for her turn to welcome me. After we had exchanged some kisses her first words were, "Are you hungry?"

"Yes, mama, I'm starving," I answered. I looked around in the familiar kitchen while mama put a place setting on the table and served some soup for me. I looked at the worn out pale green furniture and the small wood or coal burning stove. I looked up at the unusually high ceiling and saw a familiar sight, the laundry drying on the clothes rack which hung up there. "Where is papa?" I asked.

"He will be home soon. He had to go to a seminar. You know, those political ones."

As I was saying, "I hope papa forgives me," he stepped through the door.

His face showed only surprise and he said coldly, "You are home finally. If I hear that you once more try to escape from the country I, personally, will report you to the authorities." At the time he believed that much in the Communist Party.

I had been very lucky once more! People who tried to escape only a couple of weeks later than we had were convicted and sentenced for years without appeal.

I corresponded with Bela in Vienna. When he learned about our unfortunate escape attempt he wanted us to try again. I wrote to him that I wouldn't do it unless I got legal permission to leave the country. I applied every year and I was rejected every time. Once a clerk even told me that I should call my fiance back instead. Bela waited for us for one and a half years and then he went to Israel by himself.

Andy was a little bit spoiled by his grandmother and was sometimes a big mouth with her. Once after some smart remark of his she warned him, "If you don't behave I'm going to get a job and you will be all alone." I didn't think she meant it but apparently she did. Andy apologized every time that he had been smart with her but he would soon forget his promise to behave.

Mama was home to take care of Andy until he was eight years of age. After that she decided that she would go to work to add some money to the household. She took a job as a cook for a well-known family in the Jewish Congress. So Andy had to be on his own. He had a key to the apartment which he wore on a chain around his neck. At lunch time he went home from school, which was within walking distance, and warmed up his lunch. The main meal was at lunch time and in workplaces you could warm up a meal brought in a special covered dish. Andy was in grade one when on Mother's Day that year he presented me with an envelope. In the envelope was a large card with Andy's photograph in the middle. His hair was pinned back with a bobby-pin so that it wouldn't fall onto his forehead. He wore a navy blue sweater over his white shirt and he smiled slightly. Across the top of the card he had printed in red letters "To my dear parents." A small red heart was attached to the card with a red string. A piece of paper was also in the envelope with some flowers drawn by Andy and he wrote the following on it,

> For my dear mother on mother's day. I wish you a very happy day from the bottom of my heart on this day. I also promise that I will not be rude to Grandma ever again. Many kisses from your loving son, Andy.

I still treasure this card with its note. Of course grandma forgave him as she always did. Andy was, as she called him, the "light of my eyes."

Now I needed a job. I tried to go back to the kindergarten where I had last worked but to my surprise I was told that they wouldn't hire me because I had tried to escape. So I had to look for something else. Almost all of the stores were in the hands of the government. Only a few were privately owned and operated. Eventually I got a job because of my studying with Andy.

Andy was in grade two and mathematics was very hard for him. I tutored him every day and I learned the multiplication table very well but Andy still had difficulty remembering the numbers. He was a good and intelligent student and when he read something only once he could recite it well. But somehow he couldn't do this with numbers. At this time I saw an advertisement for a cashier in the newspaper. It was a nationalized hardware store that needed a cashier and I went to apply. The head bookkeeper interviewed me. When he finally asked me some questions about the multiplication table of course I was very good with it. "How do you know this subject so well?" he asked me in surprise. "Usually ladies are not very good with the multiplication table." When I told him that I had to study it with my son he laughed and hired me.

For the first couple of years in this job I was a substitute cashier. I had to go to different stores to replace the steady cashier who was either sick or on vacation. I also had to do the entire administration of the store. I did not have an adding machine and I had to add long columns of numbers but I learned my job very well. I was rewarded a few times for my good work. During this period we also had to attend political seminars but I was not a member of the Party.

Andy behaved better with his grandfather than he did with his grandmother. He adored his grandpa and almost every night grandpa usually went to bed early and let Andy lay beside him and told him stories. The stories, grandpa's own fabrications, were about a huge ship where Andy was the captain and this ship was involved in so much mischief and so many adventures! This storytelling went on until Andy was eight or nine years old. Grandpa also took him skating and swimming and to many sporting events.

In the summer my father-in-law was the director of a beautiful, huge outdoor swimming pool called "Palatinus." It was built on Margaret Island which stretched into the Danube River on the Buda side and it had four pools. One was very big with cool water; another had warm mineral water; another pool was for children and had lukewarm water; and the fourth had artificial waves. Every hour a bell was rung by pulling a rope which meant that the artificial waves were coming up. Andy was allowed to pull the bell rope and as a little boy he was so proud to do such an important job! At the sound of the bell the whole crowd would start to run in the direction of the special pool where they jumped into the waves. It was funny to watch the pool full of people as they went up and down, up and down for about fifteen minutes on the huge waves. Around the poolside were grass and benches and there were also snack bars, restaurants and souvenir shops. It was a favourite place not only for locals but for visitors from outside as well. People spent entire days at these outdoor pools. Budapest had many of them and all had natural mineral water but not all of them were so big.

Through these years I still corresponded with Bela who already been in Israel for some time. He had never married. I was very much alone and there were no decent men whom I could date. They were all married by now and I missed Bela. I still was not in love with him but he was a good human being who had been very good to Andy and me.

The enterprise where I worked had a summer resort on the bank of the Danube. It was a couple of long buildings with small, separate cottages. Each of these had a little porch in front similar to a motel. There was a common dining room and we ate our meals there. Some summers I spent my two week vacation there with Andy and the price asked by the management of my hardware store was very reasonable. I remember one summer in particular when I pretended that our little cabin was my own apartment and I didn't have to share with anybody but my son. We swam a lot and sunbathed and went to the nightly entertainment provided by the management. I got closer to my colleagues and made friends with some of them. Andy was then eleven or twelve and he also found friends in his age group.

One afternoon during this vacation at the resort my son came to me and said in a low voice, "Mother, promise me that you won't punish me for what I did."

"What did you do, Andy? Why should you deserve punishment?" I asked.

"Just promise first, then I'll tell you."

"Okay, I promise that whatever you did is over and I won't punish you."

"I swam across the Danube," he told me.

"Oh my God! That was very dangerous! Who was with you?"

"Nobody." I didn't punish him as I had promised and I was glad that nothing bad had happened to him after his dangerous act. The river was wide and fast-flowing and not even an adult dared to swim across it without an escort. This was not the first time that Andy wanted to prove his ability to do something all by himself.

My sister, Aranka, had a bungalow in the outskirts of Budapest. My son was only a little over four years old when Aranka invited him to their home for a week or so. She enrolled Andy in a local kindergarten during his visit and let him go with a six-year-old boy. She said that the older boy was very reliable and there was no reason to be afraid. They had to cross a busy road. One day, to Aranka's surprise, Andy arrived home earlier than usual. "Why are you home early?" asked my sister.

"I just escaped through the big gate because I wanted to come alone without Peter," he replied. My sister spanked him hard for this act. The next day the teacher told my sister that she shouldn't punish the child just because he wanted to prove his independence.

After that swim in the river Andy promised me he would not do any more wild things. The vacation over we went back to our daily routine. I now worked steadily on one store on Rakoczi Street which was a main street in Budapest and a short distance from our apartment. Andy, in addition to his school, went to swimming training every day. He was a good swimmer and was being trained for the next Olympics. Occasionally he went twice a day to practise, early in the morning before school started and also after school. Sometimes, when it was a cold winter day and I didn't want him to go, I didn't wake him in the morning. Still, Andy would wake himself up and hurry off to his training. I once went to watch him compete in a race in a big pool. During the race a lady behind me said to her partner, "Look at that little boy in the red cap how good and fast he is!"

Bursting with pride I turned to them and said, "He is my son!"

One day a friend of the store manager came into the store.

He introduced himself to me and said a few words. He didn't stay long but after closing I found him waiting for me outside. He asked if he could walk me home. I agreed and after that he came to the store often and started to court me. I didn't know much about him. He told me he was divorced but I noticed that he had a very sharp brain and that he was highly educated. It was much later that I found out that he was a gambler.

He went to the race track every time he had a couple of forints to spend. When he won he showered me with presents but sometimes he borrowed money from me. On one cold winter day when we met after the store closed he hadn't worn a winter coat. He had sold it to get some money for his awful habit. My in-laws knew about this friendship and they were very much against it. Sometimes I didn't see him for months and then he would show up again. One day he asked me to marry him. I hesitated. I was very much alone and very much longed for a home of my own and my own family life. But Emil didn't have a steady job and he was a gambler. On top of this he and Andy hated each other. I refused his proposal but we still dated.

The revolution and second escape

It was a warm autumn day on the 23rd of October 1956 when we in the store heard singing and marching coming from the streets. We all hurried outside to investigate.

Hungary had been under Russian occupation since the Second World War and the people of Hungary were fed up. They were getting rebellious and wanted to free themselves from this occupation. The marchers in the street were university students who had started a peaceful demonstration against the Russians. It was afternoon. By the evening the crowd had become much bigger. Like an avalanche it got uglier and more violent as the days went by. In the next few days the protesters stole as many weapons as they could and opened the gates of the jails. Then the mob started on the Jews again. They even put posters on the walls saying, "You Jews don't have to go to Auschwitz. We will kill you right here." I couldn't believe that hardly ten years had passed since the war when we Jews were killed by the millions. It was a terrible, shameful sin and now they started on us again. But no, not again! I would not let them do what they had done to us in 1944!

The attempted revolution went on and on until the government asked for more troops from Russia to help defeat it. The Soviets came and tanks were soon roaming the streets. Some Hungarian youths as young as twelve and thirteen made molotov cocktails and threw them at the tanks. My in-laws and I had a hard time keeping Andy in the house. He wanted to go out to meet his friends; God knows what he wanted to do. One day two very young Russian soldiers, they weren't more than eighteen years of age, came to our apartment. We were on street level and the very first door in the courtyard. The soldiers asked for some water. Fortunately papa, who spoke seven Slavic languages, understood what they wanted and he gave them a few glasses of water to drink. They were so frightened at first. The two soldiers had poked their rifles into the open door before they entered. I felt very sorry for them.

Another day Andy and some other children from the build-

ing were playing in the yard collecting empty shell cartridges
from the grounds. A few older Russian soldiers came in and
because Andy was the tallest of the boys the soldier said
"daway" and wanted to take my son away. I only saw the incident through the window and thought that they were only talking. Andy also knew some Russian because it was a compul-
sory subject in his school. He told me later that the soldiers
saw the cartridges in his hand and that this was the reason that
they wanted to take him. But, he showed them that the
cartridges were empty and he was only playing with them
with the other children so they let him go.

The whole country was in turmoil. The beautiful city of
Budapest was in ruins once more. There was no electricity for
days and the stores were closed. People broke into them and
plundered all over the city. I couldn't go to work for a week or
so. It was not safe to be on the streets at all.

After the revolution was defeated people started to escape
from the country. We all listened to the messages on the "Radio Free Europe" station; messages from people who already
were abroad. They encouraged their friends and relatives to
follow them. Those messages encouraged me to decide to go.
I discussed it with my in-laws. They both agreed. Papa, who
once wanted to report me for my first escape, now said, "Go
my daughter. Go anywhere you can just far away from here."
He had become very bitterly disappointed in the Communist
Party.

Mama also approved of my plan but she was crying as she
asked, "Will I see my grandson, the light of my eyes, ever
again?"

"Yes mama, you will," I said as I hugged her, almost crying
myself.

On a cold November night I approached my son to ask him,
"What would you say, Andy, if I said let's go to the West and
start a new life?"

"Are you serious, mother?" he asked me. "You want me to
leave my friends, school, teachers, my swimming training
and my grandparents behind?"

"Yes my dear. If you want to come with me you will have to

do all those things. But I won't force you."

"All right, mother, but why? Why do you want to leave our country?" he asked. I pulled my son close to me, put my arms around his shoulders and explained it to him in a few sentences. "During the war you were only a two-year-old baby. We were lucky to be taken to the ghetto, even though many of us died of hunger, sickness or by shooting. You also were near to death because you were very ill and there was no doctor, no medicine and no food. And all those things happened to us because we are Jews. You also know that is the reason your daddy was killed. Right now we are in the middle of the Revolution and I don't want the same thing to happen to us again. Now we have our chance to escape and to start a new and peaceful life somewhere else." Andy was convinced. As a matter of fact it was a big adventure for him and he got very excited. But there were a couple of worrisome questions remaining: how and with whom could I arrange our escape?

I phoned Emil who was not supposed to come to our home because of my in-laws. We met and I mentioned my plan to him and asked his help or advice. It turned out that he also wanted to escape later the same week because time was running out for the dissidents. He told me where to go.

In the last week of November of 1956 Andy and I said goodbye to mama and papa. I told them that we were going to join a group, which was true, but I didn't mention that Emil was among them. I was too busy with my problems and future even to think about how terrible was the heartache and sorrow mama and papa must have felt when their beloved and only grandchild and I left forever. Just recently I found a box of old letters dating back to 1957. There were letters from Bela, from a girlfriend of mine, from Andy's favourite teacher, a young woman, Marta Beke, a cousin on my father's side, a letter from my sister Elizabeth and some letters from papa. Elizabeth's letter was a long one and among many things she wrote:

I went to see your in-laws today. It was terrible to see your papa crying in his bed and mama sitting in the corner on her favourite little stool crying her heart out. I went to kiss and comfort them. I told them that you both are all right and that is what all of you wanted, a safer and better future. I promised to see them often. They calmed down a little and papa told me in a shaking voice that if they had been younger they would have gone with you and Andy.

We met with the group in the Keleti Railway Station and wanted to go by train to Vienna. We boarded the train but had to change after a few hours in a city to another train to Vienna. But before we could change trains we were captured by the Russians. At the station we were separated from the group. We all split into twos and threes. Andy, Emil and I were sitting on a bench when two Russian soldiers came over. When they asked were we were going Andy told them that we were going to visit relatives in Vienna. Of course they didn't believe this and ordered us to return to Budapest. Luckily they didn't arrest us and when we promised to go back they left us alone.

We didn't return but hid in a small hotel and tried again the next morning. This time we were lucky. After many kilometers on foot and a long train ride we arrived in Vienna. When our little group got off the train it was night and we didn't know where to go so we walked to the first policeman we saw and informed him that we were Hungarian refugees. He took us to the nearest police station and put us in a cell for the night. It brought back unpleasant memories to be in jail again. I knew that it was different this time because they were only providing shelter for the night. The next morning we went to the authorities where we were registered and helped in every way. They placed us in hotels and camps and gave us money, food and free transportation. We were helped by the Jewish Congress in Vienna as well. We stayed in the city for four weeks and Andy had a good time exploring it.

Papa had a brother-in-law there and papa had given us his address just in case. He was an awfully bitter old man who still mourned his only child, a ten-year-old daughter, and his wife who had been taken to Auschwitz and killed. The man's wife was papa's only sister. I saw Karl only once but Andy spent a lot of time with him and almost every day ate lunch or supper with him. We also went to see a schoolmate of mama's, auntie Elsa, and she also was nice to us.

In contrast to Budapest, which was in darkness and in ruins when we left, Vienna was gorgeous! There were lights, many lights, beautiful buildings and friendly people. I felt so emancipated, so happy. It seemed as if I was just starting to live again without fear. I recall a few lovely episodes during our stay in Vienna.

One day Andy and I were walking on a sidewalk eating doughnuts and a friendly policeman greeted us from this post in the middle of the road with a loud, "Gut appetit!"

I shouted back, "Danke schoen!" On occasion we needed a small household item and when the store owner learned that we were refugees he gave it to us free. I also remember a very unusual but wonderful scene which once more involved a policeman. A few days before Christmas I saw a policeman at his usual position directing traffic from his small platform in the middle of the road. Around his feet was a pile of gifts in the form of parcels which he received from drivers who passed him daily!

We, like most of our fellow refugees, wanted to go to the United States of America. We spent an entire night in front of the United States embassy in Vienna waiting for admittance but the wait was to no avail. Only those who had relatives in the States were able to emigrate there. Then we heard that Canada would take us without any discrimination so we applied.

On 27 December 1956 Andy and I and Emil sailed in a huge ship called "Berlin." It was a luxury ship with some two thousand passengers and only two hundred Hungarians. Again, Andy enjoyed the journey very much. He found some sports activities on board like swimming and tennis but I was seasick most of the time. We were at sea for eleven days and arrived in Halifax on 8 January 1957. I still have our tickets which cost the Canadian government $175.00 each.

We arrived in Halifax in the morning and we were escorted to the Immigration Hall where all two hundred of us were given a paper shopping bag with a handle, something we didn't have at home. Paper was very precious in Hungary and when we went shopping we usually took our own bags. Here in Halifax we received some necessary things in our shopping bags, like a towel, tooth brush, soap and such. We also got five dollars each, the first Canadian money I had ever seen. I didn't see any of Halifax only some deep snow and some workers with unusual and heavy overboots. After coffee and doughnuts we were taken into a room for a medical examination and x-rays. On the same day we all boarded a train for Winnipeg.

This was the first time that we had travelled in a train with sleeping facilities. We were fascinated when at night a porter made our seats into couches on which we could sleep. He also put covers on them for us. It was also the first time that we were lost without the English language because until this point we had always had an Hungarian interpreter. I remember an ocassion when we needed a washroom. I took out my little Hungarian-English dictionary which I had bought in Vienna. It was only a pocket-size dictionary with a few pages. I looked up "washroom" and showed it to the porter. He pointed in the direction where it was located. I stepped into a room but didn't see any sign of toilet facilities, only some doors with mirrors on them. I went back and looked up the word "where" and showed it to the man. He smiled and escorted me right into the lady's washroom.

In our new country, Canada

Again, only those people who had relatives in the two major cities were allowed to go to Montreal and Toronto. We travelled another seventy-two hours and on a very cold day we arrived at our destination in our adopted country. The temperature was 40 degrees below zero. We had never experienced such cold and we were shivering in our thin coats and shoes.

However, people once more were nice to us. We were given warm clothes and many other things we needed. We stayed in the Immigration Hall in Winnipeg for three weeks. They served us white bread, the type for toasting, with our meal and I was soon desperate thinking that in Canada they didn't have any other type of bread, only this which tasted like pastry. While still in the Immigration Hall we began to learn to speak English. I wanted to learn the language very much. I felt so stupid without it.

One bright, sunny day my son asked my permission to go outdoors. "You can go out, Andy, but don't forget to put on your cap, the one I knitted for you back home."

"But mother! Look out the window. See how sunny and wonderful it is outside!" he insisted.

"I know it looks gorgeous but it is awfully cold," I reminded him.

"I don't need one," Andy said and putting on his thin coat he ran out of the building. In five minutes he was back inside the Immigration Hall. Both his ears were frozen and his hands and feet were like blocks of ice.

After three weeks in the Immigration Hall the government and the Jewish Family Services helped us until I was on my own. The Jewish Congress rented a basement apartment for us. It contained a bedroom and a fairly big kitchen. The shower and toilet were in the furnace room. It was a nice bungalow near to the Red River and there was a very nice park nearby. The owners of the house were an elderly couple who originated from Russia. The lady never learned to say my first name properly. Despite my frequent correction she always called me Iba instead of Ibi which was the shortened form of my name used by everyone who knew me.

Sometimes the owner of the house came through our kitchen to go to his apartment upstairs. I thought he used to go that way and just forgot that the basement was now rented. He didn't even say hello but just walked through. Another inconvenience stemmed from the work habits of the lady of the house. She slept through half the day and did her housework late at night. Several times I woke up because of the sound of her footsteps and of her cleaning. One day I tried to explain to her that I just couldn't sleep because of her activities which sometimes ran as late as three in the morning. She promised that she would write letters instead!

From the Jewish Congress we got some second hand furniture, bedding, pots, pans, plates and other necessities. Andy slept in the kitchen on a cot and I slept in the small bedroom. Despite the disturbances from upstairs I was very happy to be in my apartment. Now I was completely on my own. My first shopping day in the nearby small supermarket was a difficult task. I could recognize things like fruit, bread, chicken or milk since it was obvious what they were but the packages and tin cans puzzled me. However, I saw a tin can in the supermarket with a picture of pancakes on it. The pancakes in the picture were covered with a liquid. "Andy would be happy to have a few pancakes," I though. "Maybe, if he doesn't like it, I just won't put this liquid on it," so I bought the tin with the picture of pancakes on it. I also needed some toothpicks but couldn't find them. I stopped a salesperson and showed him with my finger pointing to my tooth what I wanted. He took me over to the counter where the toothbrushes were kept. I went back to the clerk said, "No." Then I did the same movement with my finger. He escorted me to the toothpastes. I gave up.

At home I opened the tin can with the pancakes in the picture and found that there was only tomato sauce in it! I learned my lesson after that. Except for one occasion when I bought a box of washing detergent with a picture of a floral printed towel on the side of the box. I was sure there was no towel in it. However, on opening the box I found to my surprise that it contained a light-blue, terry-cotton towel with blue flowers. I was delighted. After that I always bought detergent with a towel printed on the box and after a while I had built a nice collection of towels.

Although I had difficulties in adjusting to my new life, in the first few months I was happy and satisfied with everything. Sometimes when I think back on those days I feel that I was happier then with my one bedroom apartment with the tiny bathroom than many years later with my own bungalow. I don't think that I can explain why that was. The feeling may have been produced because of the circumstances I had left in Hungary where I never had my own home and I was very dependent on my in-laws.

In Winnipeg there were a great many Ukrainian people. The women wore colourful printed wool kerchiefs and they dressed somehow differently from us. They had poor taste in dressing: they mixed many colours, something which was a "no no" for me. I simply thought that this was the Canadian way of dressing. Another thing I noticed was the behaviour of youths which was different from our own youngsters. I recall an episode on the bus which, on this occasion, was crowded when an elderly man stepped on. He was standing, supporting himself on his cane when a woman, who was not very young, stood up to offer her seat. Two teenage girls started to laugh when they saw this kind gesture. They had no idea that they should have offered their own seats. Andy jumped up from his seat whenever an older person entered the bus. Finally he said to me, "Mother, I'm not sitting down even if there is a seat because I would just have to stand up again to give it to an older person." So he just stood during bus rides. Now, Canadian youths are more polite to their elders than they were in those days.

Andy was enroled at a school in Winnipeg in grade eight as he had been in Hungary. Unfortunately, after a couple of months Andy was put back to the sixth grade because he did not know the language. He was heartbroken and it took me a long time to reassure him that in a year he would catch up with his class. In a letter his teacher in Hungary sent in July of 1957 she wrote:

I hope, my dear, that by the end of the year you get used to the school and you make some friends. As I know your ability, I'm sure that your are going to be among the first students very soon. Among your old classmates, five of them have left the country with their parents. Those who stayed are studying diligently. You do the same to make yours and your mother's life easier. I always think of you fondly as one of my best students.

Andy was happy about his favourite teacher's letter and it helped him a lot.

When the Jewish community learned that I was a widow with a young boy they helped us even more. Sometimes, when I got home from work, I found a box at our doorstep full of warm clothes for Andy. On another occasion a man who owned an electrical shop gave Andy a radio and another one presented him with a record player and some records. All of them were total strangers.

My first job was in a men's clothing factory. I was taken to the factory by a social worker and I was hired as a sewing machine operator. I had to learn so many things, including the language, at the same time. The sewing machines were so monstrous and it was hard to learn to operate them. I had to sew trouser pockets and after a short time I had to do them as piece work. I earned $26.00 a week including overtime. To live on that salary for the two of us I had to be very money wise. I used some envelopes to keep my rent, grocery and spending money separate. I even managed to give Andy some allowance out of my paycheque. Still, it is true that at that time for ten dollars a person could buy a week's worth of groceries.

I went to night school twice a week and I was the most diligent student in the whole class. I made some Hungarian friends and we got together on weekends and at night to study English. When it was my turn to receive my friends one of us always had to hold one of the legs of the table otherwise it would collapse.

In the first few weeks in Winnipeg Emil wanted to marry me. Fortunately, we had to have been in the country for a certain amount of time to get permission for marriage. After a few months he started to court a rich Jewish girl. He spoke Yiddish fluently so it wasn't difficult for them to communicate. They got married and I was glad that it turned out this way because he still disliked my son. However, after about a year they were divorced. After the divorce he came to see me again. "What happened? How come you want to see me after you told me you dislike my son?" I asked him.

"I think that Andy has grown and probably changed so we could marry," he replied.

"No, my son hasn't changed and please leave me alone. Even if I would have married you originally I wouldn't do it after you left me for another woman." He stayed in Winnipeg for a while and then he left the city.

In our eyes Winnipeg looked like a big village. The small, coloured houses were like weekend cottages at Lake Balaton in Hungary. But the Hudson Bay Company was very impressive and I enjoyed the huge selection of dresses, lingerie and just about everything else. Also, in the grocery stores, I could chose many, many foods. One day after work I went to buy groceries. There were so many types of cheese to choose from but I couldn't read the label and I didn't know which one to buy. I choose one anyway and on the bus going home I smelled an awful odour, like someone hadn't washed his feet for weeks. I looked around in the bus but couldn't tell who the guilty one was. But the odour escorted me home and only when I opened my grocery bag did I notice that the awful smell came from the cheese I had bought. I put it in the oven to hide it.

When the weather permitted Andy and I would go for a stroll on our street and my son's pastime was, for every car we saw, to tell me what type it was. I was fascinated by his cleverness with cars. One day he asked me, "Mother, do you know when we are going to be rich?"

"No, when?" I replied.

"When we have soft drinks in our home every day and when I have a real bed and not this narrow cot on which I always bruise myself." I promised him that we were going to be that rich some day.

We corresponded with my in-laws regularly. I wrote them every month and their first letter arrived on 8 February 1957. Their one-page airmail letter was written in such tiny letters that I had to strain my eyes to read it. Here is a section from that letter which I still keep.

Our heart is still very heavy but we were glad to read that you are both all right. Your first letter was really interesting and we showed it to everybody who asked about you and Andy. Mama and I hope that you both will have a secure and more peaceful life than here at home. I have some questions to ask. Which way did you go and with whom? How long did the journey last? When did you reach the border? I hope neither of you were cold because here it was very cold at that time. Did you have enough money? Here everybody says that Canada is a good country and everybody could make a living there if they have work. I know that in all your life you were a diligent worker and I'm sure you will do your best to provide all the necessities for you and Andy. Please write every tiny detail about your life, your health, your work and learning the new language. What do you do in your spare time? Do you have any friends?

Our home is so quiet and empty without you and Andy. The only joy we have is when you write to us. Imagine that my little budgie, Pityu, asks all the time "Where is Ibi and Andy?" It greets every customer with, "Good day." You know that I'm working at home now and my patients are increasing.

The ruins are all cleaned up and the city is starting to look like before the revolution. The electricity is restored and the movies and theatres are playing again.

After a few months I was transferred to another factory. That was for women's clothing. There I found some malicious people and I remember some unpleasant experiences. I was sewing a black skirt with red lining and I sewed it completely with the wrong-coloured thread. One of the workers noticed my mistake but she waited until I had finished my work and then she went to the forelady and told her about my mistake. I had to take the entire skirt apart and do it over again with the right thread.

The other episode was awfully shameful for me. There was a machine in the factory which sold bottled soft drinks for ten cents. I saw empty bottles all over the place and believing that the cleaning staff would throw them in the garbage can I collected them and took them home. Andy redeemed them in the grocery store for two cents apiece. The next morning I felt terribly embarrassed when the forelady came over and told me that I was not supposed to take the bottles home because the owner reused them in the machine.

Andy also had difficulties in school. He had yet to make any friends and he was very homesick. One afternoon when I arrived home Andy was sitting on a chair bending down pretending that he was busy with his shoelaces. When for my greeting he didn't look up I asked him "What are you hiding, Andy? Why don't you look up?" Then he looked at me and I saw black and bloody bruises all over his face. "Oh my God! What happened to you?"

Andy told me that he had a fight with a boy who said, "Stinky Jew" to him.

"On no! Not again! Not here!" I cried out hugging him and kissing his bruised face.

"But you should see, mother, what I did to him! His bruises are worse than mine. And the teacher was on my side because I just reacted to the boy's remark." I felt so miserable and terribly sorry for my son. I washed his face and tried to assure him and myself as well that it was only an isolated incident.

Another night when we arrived home Andy turned on the little radio. Suddenly the whole apartment was full of beautiful music by the famous composer, Johann Strauss. Andy cried out, "Mother! Mother, do you hear it? A Hungarian song!" He laughed and cried with joy. It didn't affect me but my heart went out to him.

"Darling," I said, "if you want to go back to your grandparents and friends I will let you go. But I wouldn't go back for anything."

"Then I would not go either," he answered.

In the early summer of 1958 we moved to another apartment. This time we had our own tiny bathroom in the apartment so we didn't have to fear any more that somebody would walk into the furnace room while Andy or I was taking a shower. Our little home was now completely self-contained. It was true that Andy still slept in the kitchen on the same cot but in the corner of the kitchen was a kitchenette with a stove and a fridge where I did my cooking. We used the kitchen, which was the biggest room, for everything. It served as the living room, dining room and study. Although the furniture was the same second hand pieces I made the little apartment as cosy and pretty as I could. I hung white lace curtains in the windows and put a lovely printed table cloth on the table and some inexpensive but colourful pictures on the walls.

In the bedroom I had a wine-coloured velvet bedspread on the bed which had been given to me and which I treasured very much. Then one day a friend came over with her little boy. I was so upset to see the child, wearing his running shoes, jump on my bedspread! I was relieved when his mother ordered him down. Every morning before work I tidied my apartment and I paused in the doorway to admire it before leaving.

One night, to celebrate our new apartment, I wanted to bake a walnut cake. I set the temperature on my nice, white, four-burner stove, whose oven had a window, the first I had ever seen. I placed my cake in the oven and after about ten minutes I noticed that the light in the oven had gone off. "Oh my God," I thought, "the oven is broken and my cake is going to be ruined. What am I going to do?" I went to my Hungarian neighbour next door to ask if I could use her oven but by the time I returned to my kitchen the light in the oven was on again. That is how I learned that that oven was automatic and that the light went off when it reached the desired temperature and turned on again when it started to warm up.

On another night Andy and I went to our first movie in Canada. It was very memorable not only because it was the first in our new country but because the movie, "The Ten Commandments," made a big impression on both of us. I also recall how beautiful everything looked when I came out of the cinema. It was early January and the Christmas lights and decorations were still up. We stopped at the first corner and I looked around at the quiet street with thick, fresh snow everywhere and the small coloured Christmas lights around the windows of the houses, on the trees and bushes. It was so peaceful and relaxing. I hugged my son and planted a kiss on his cheek.

"Are you all right, mother?" he asked me.

"Yes, my son, I am." How could he understand what I felt being free of every bad thing of my past?

Across from our apartment on the same floor was another Hungarian couple. They were about ten years younger than I but despite the age difference we became good friends. The woman, Ady, also worked in a clothing factory and her husband, Eugene, worked in a bakery. Eugene had a positive influence on Andy. He learned to do some housework from him because Eugene worked during the night and after sleeping until about two p.m. in the afternoon he did some cooking or similar work in the house. They became good friends and Eugene was like a big brother to Andy.

In our first summer in Canada in 1957 Andy, as a gift to him from the Jewish Congress, was sent to a camp for the entire summer. The camp, near Kenora, was called "Lake of the Woods." When we received the list of clothes for him to take to camp a funny incident occurred. After Andy had finished reading the list to me he said, "Mother, I understand that I need all those things in the camp but I'm puzzled about one thing."

"What is that," I asked him?

"I don't know why I should need rubber pyjamas!" I started to laugh because I knew it was a misunderstanding which was connected to a Hungarian word. On the list of items needed were cotton pyjamas. In Hungarian the word *Coton* was a trademark name for *condom*. Andy knew that a condom was made from rubber and seeing the words *cotton pyjamas* he thought they also must be made of rubber. After I explained his misunderstanding he also had a good laugh.

Despite the language barrier Andy had a very nice time at the camp. He had always had a charming way with girls and women and they liked him and this partially helped to ensure him a good time. Also, after half a year in the country he already knew enough to communicate with other children.

My first outing came when a couple took me to the camp one Sunday to visit Andy. The woman picked me up at my home and drove me to their beautiful house early in the morning. In their marvellous white kichen she fixed lots of sandwiches and other food to take with us. We went by car, my first ride ever in an automobile, and I enjoyed the beautiful countryside and weather very much because otherwise in Winnipeg the weather was very unpredictable. I remember on one occasion it was a nice spring day in the middle of May when I went to work dressed lightly. However, when I came out of the factory late in the afternoon it took me one and a half hours for the normal half-hour bus ride home because of the snow storm!

On this occasion the weather behaved and Andy was so happy to see me. He showed me his cabin, his new friends and also he happily told me that he was able to swim in the lake, this for the first time since he had left Hungary. Besides being a good swimmer, Andy was also a good dancer. Once he was invited to a dance party by a classmate. The girl's father came to our little apartment with his pretty daughter to pick Andy up. They knew that we were refugees and couldn't yet speak the language but these things didn't matter for them.

My son also liked to take photographs just like his daddy did. Andy worked after school as a delivery boy in a drug-store. He delivered by bicycle for fifty cents an hour. During the summer of 1958 he worked as a warehouse packer and earned $42.00 a week. I gave him back some allowance and he saved it to buy a camera. He bought it for $28.00 which was more than I earned in a week.

Because I was a widow all of my friends were looking for a husband for me. One of my classmates in night school, an elderly lady, talked about a man, rich she said, who wanted to marry. When I asked her how old this gentleman was she said that he was 45 years old, the right age for me. Finally I agreed to meet him. He phoned me first and then on the same night he came to pick me up in his car. My first impression was that he was much older than his described years. We went to a coffee shop for a cup of coffee but before we went in he gave me a ten-cent chocolate bar for my son. He talked about his business, he owned a delicatessen, and how busy he was. He was so busy that for fifteen years he hadn't had a vacation. I didn't like him.

I asked him (I didn't know it wasn't polite) how old he was and he admitted 65 which was a 25 years difference between us. And also, which we couldn't communicate properly because of our language differences. I never went on another date with him after this first one. When my classmate wanted to introduce someone else I thanked her and told her that I wasn't interested.

Andy's operation

Among our Hungarian friends in Canada there was a young medical doctor whom we knew from Budapest. One late spring night in 1958 he came to visit us with his wife. Andy happily read the letter to them which he had just received from his grandparents. Suddenly, his voice cracked and he felt strong pain in his throat. Our friend Steven, the doctor, examined him and the more he touched Andy's neck the more serious his face became. Finally he said that I had to take Andy to the hospital first thing in the morning. The next morning I took him to St. Boniface Hospital where Steven worked as in intern. I was told by the doctors that Andy had to stay a few days for further examination. Follwing this the doctor in charge told me that he must operate on Andy. They had found a small tumour the size of a grape in his thyroid which was full of liquid. The pain that Andy had felt while reading was the tumour which had burst open. They had to remove it.

By this time I was working in my third and final job in Winnipeg, in a factory called Sport-Ease Fashions Ltd. The atmosphere in this factory was pleasant and I didn't have to do piecework. I received sixty cents an hour and if I worked Saturdays I earned enough to live on. My boss and his wife were from Austria. I think they had been Canada for a long time already so they hadn't suffered the Holocaust. The boss was especially nice to me.

Andy's operation was scheduled for eight a.m. on the fifth day of his hospitalization. Steven promised me that he would phone as soon as it was over. I hardly slept during the night for I had nobody there who could be with me in that terrible time. I told myself over and over again that Andy would be all right, that he was young and healthy, that the tumour would not be malignant and that very soon we would forget his illness completely.

It was better to go to work but I couldn't keep my mind on my work. I sewed a piece then I took it apart. I took apart more pieces than I sewed. I waited for the telephone call all morning. The time passed very slowly and there was no call. I was running back and forth between the washroom and my sewing machine. What had happened? Ten o'clock, ten-thirty, eleven o'clock and nothing. I will not look at my watch again, I promised myself. But I did and it was only a quarter after eleven. At eleven-thirty the telephone rang. I jumped up and before they called my name I was heading for the office. The call was for me. At the other end of the line I heard Steven's calm and friendly voice. "Everything is okay," he said. "I didn't call you earlier because I wanted to hear Andy talk to be sure that there was no damage to his voice." Tears were pouring down my cheeks as I listened to what Steven had to say. "The doctors had to remove a portion of the thyroid because the tumour was planted in it," my friend continued. "Andy is going to be all right, the tumour was not malignant. You can come to see him now." My boss, seeing my tears, was very concerned. I assured him that my tears were from happiness because my son was going to be all right soon.

St. Boniface Hospital was in the outskirts of Winnipeg. After a long ride and many questions about the whereabouts of the hospital I finally arrived at Andy's bedside. He was very pale and had a thick dressing and he was still sleeping. I took his hand in mine and talked to him soothingly. He opened his eyes occasionally and gently squeezed my hand. The third day after his operation Andy felt good and hungry. He ate everything brought for him including the untouched food of the other adult patient's in his room. He was back to school in about two weeks.

My sister, Elizabeth, and her family went to Israel with legal papers in the summer of 1957. In her first letter in September of that same year she wrote that they were bitterly sorry to have made that move. Here is an excerpt from her letter,

We got two rooms, I should say two small cubicles in a settlement with a shower. We got three beds, one table, two chairs, one pot, two cups and cutlery, and a small petroleum stove for cooking if I had the food for it. There is no electricity in the entire settlement and around us there are big stones that make it very hard to walk to the bus station which is about twenty minutes away under an awfully hot sun. We got some money for starting out but I already have sold Feri's electric shaver in the city to live on for a little while longer. There are no Hungarians among our neighbours; they are from Iraq, Morocco and from Poland and we can't communicate with them.

When in her next letter Elizabeth wrote that a very much treasured chicken of hers was stolen by a hungry stray cat and she had been crying all day long I decided to send them a parcel.

I though that I was in a much better situation even though I also struggled for our living in Winnipeg. I put together a package which contained instant coffee, sugar, bittersweet chocolate candy, canned foods, coffee beans, and even toys for Tomi. At the same time I wrote a letter to say that the parcel was on its way. Their reply to the parcel came in April 1958. Elizabeth wrote that they were incredibly happy for the goodies and that I should have seen Tomi's joy at getting all those toys and chocolates. Tomi also wrote a whole page in his mother's letter thanking me for his presents and telling us that he already spoke a little of the Hebrew language, *Ivrit*. He asked how Andy was after the operation and how his studies in English were going. It was a nice letter from a not quite ten-year-old.

In Toronto

In the late summer of 1958 we decided to move to Toronto. Andy learned he had two classmates there from Hungary and also my other sister, Aranka, and her family, had moved to Toronto from Hamilton. Aranka and her husband, Jeno, their daughter Marianna and her husband Laci had left Hungary on 24 December 1956. Jeno had had a position in the Ministry of Architecture in Budapest and had been a member of the Communist Party. However, because of his big mouth, he was very outspoken and talked against the Party despite his friends' warning and he was eventually expelled from the Party. After his expulsion he was accused of being an enemy of the regime. Jeno felt that he and his family were in danger so they decided to escape also. They too travelled via Austria. They travelled to the Austrian border to a village where Jeno hired a local man who would take them across. After they reached the border on foot the man wanted to return but Jeno gave him an additional bottle of rum to escort them right across.

On the Austrian side of the border all of the Hungarian escapees took rest and refuge in big haystacks which were scattered all over the field at that point. Aranka and her family joined another family with a small child at the base of a haystack. The child was almost lifeless from the cold and Aranka thought he was already frozen to death. Jeno took out another small bottle of rum from his coat pocket and poured a few drops into the child's mouth several times. This probably saved the child's life.

The Austrian authorities knew about the Hungarian refugees and they sent border guards to search and to pick them up. They were then taken by horse carriage to the nearest villange and from there they were moved to Vienna. After staying there for several weeks they arrived in Halifax in the first week of March 1957. They also went through medical examination there and, unfortunately, the x-ray showed a spot on Aranka's lung. My sister and Jeno were transferred to a sanatorium in Hamilton where Jeno got a job as a cleaner. They stayed there for six months. During this time the frequent x-rays showed that the spot neither grew nor moved so Aranka had probably had it from birth. The doctors released her. I eventually learned of their wheareabouts in Canada from mama's letter from Hungary.

We decided to fly to Toronto at the end of August so Andy could go to school in September. I told my plans to my boss who was very understanding and they even invited us for a Sabbath supper on the last Friday night before our departure. They presented us with a lovely gift of two silver candleholders. I was very moved. With my broken English I thanked them and promised to light the Sabbath candles every Friday night Until this moment I hadn't done this. Also from my colleagues I received a leather handbag as a going-away present. Never before had I received any presents in my workplace. My boss also wrote a letter of recommendation.

August 22nd, 1958.

To whom it may concern:

This is to certify that Mrs. Ibolya Reti has been in our employ for the past year as a Sewing Machine Operator and her work has been satisfactory at all times.

    She is a very reliable and conscientious worker and our very best wishes accompany her.

Sport-Ease Fashions Ltd.,

(signature)

E. Albersheim,
Pres.

We said goodbye to our friends and the next Sunday my doctor friend, Steven and his wife, drove us to the airport. After arriving at the Toronto airport we went by bus to the terminal where Aranka and her family (husband, daughter, and son-in-law), were waiting for us. My savings of $300.00 were divided in two places. The money inlcuded Andy's salary from his summer vacation which he gave me to start our life in Toronto. I put half of the money in a handbag and the other half in my purse.

    When we arrived at the bus station our parcels were taken from the bus and put on the sidewalk. Everybody picked a parcel and the one with the money was left behind! We went to Aranka's place where we spent a night. I understood that she had a small place but she put the mattress from the bed on the floor and we slept on it. Next morning I noticed my loss. I was so very upset and I cried. I needed the money to rent a home and to buy food until I got a job. My niece, Marianna, phoned the station and she was told that there was a blue handbag still there and she could come to pick it up. What a relief! My first impression of Toronto was of gratefulness.

The next day Andy and I went apartment hunting. I needed Andy for two reasons. He spoke the language more fluently than I and he had a good sense of direction which I have never had. He had said to me, "Mother, if you want to go somewhere, always turn in the opposite direction you originally thought to go." I tried it and it worked!

We started out in the morning around Kensington Market because I was told that rent was more reasonable there. We saw many "Flat To Let" signs in windows but by early afternoon we still had had no luck. Either they didn't want teenagers or refused us because I had no job yet. We got hungry and tired. When we saw a grocery store we went in. It happened to be owned by an Hungarian. I bought a quarter pound of salami and some bread. There was a small playground nearby where we sat on a bench and ate our lunch hungrily from the paper in which it was wrapped.

Finally, we found and rented a flat near Aranka's place on Cumberland Avenue. It contained two small furnished rooms and a kitchen. We had to share the bathroom with the owner and his family. Again, we had no privacy because we couldn't lock our door from the outside. There was only a latch inside. My brother-in-law helped me get a job as a cleaning lady in the Western Hospital where he worked as an orderly. He had a doctorate in agriculture but without the English language he was glad to get any job.

I had been told that we might get some help from the Welfare Department for our new beginning so Andy and I went there to inquire. There we met a couple who had come from Vancouver at the same time as we had come from Winnipeg and who were also Hungarian. We started to talk and when the woman asked where my husband was I told her that I was a widow. Her next question was, "Would you consider re-marrying?"

"Yes, I would if I could find a suitable man."

"I know just the right man for you," Mary, my new friend, told me, "He was a comrade of my husband in the labour camp in Hungary. He is a bachelor, forty-six years old and very hard-working. He is honest, clean and a handsome person but he is from a small village in Hungary so he is not a city person like you." I was interested and Mary gave me her phone number to call her when I had a chance.

Andy enrolled in the Central Technical School on Harbord Street. He met some of his schoolmates from Budapest and was much happier than in Winnipeg. He made some new friends as well and he still maintains a friendship with one of them.

The next week I started my new job in the hospital. I got a uniform, a blue dress, and I washed floors and toilets. After a while I was promoted and my new uniform was then a light brown with a green hem and neck and a half apron also with green around the edge. I didn't wash floors any more but cleaned the patients' rooms and their toilets. I did this work for two years. During all that time I studied English hoping that some day I would get a more suitable job for myself.

One night, while cleaning my handbag, I found the phone number of my new girlfriend, Mary. I called her up. "Hello, Mary, it's Ibi. Remember we met at the Welfare Department in August?"

"Oh yes, I remember. How are you?"

"I'm fine, thank you, Mary. I'm working in a hospital. Remember you asked me if I would consider remarrying and if so that you would have a man for me?"

"Of course I remember. I already have mentioned you to that man and he wants to meet you very much." As I have said, Mary and her husband had come from Vancouver to be with their long time friends in Toronto. We set up a date for me to meet Mary's friend at the apartment of these friends, Ica and Tibi. This was for the following Sunday at three in the afternoon. I was very curious about both the looks and the character of the man I was about to meet.

I dressed carefully in my best outfit which I had received in

Winnipeg as a handout. It was a black suit with a white blouse. They were in good condition and fitted me perfectly. I fixed my thick, dark hair and put some lipstick on. I never used any other make-up. I wore a pair of knee high nylons. I remember pulling my skirt down a few times to cover my knees as I was sitting across from my date. He later joked that he married me because he liked my knees.

When I arrived at the given address the hosts, Ica and Tibi, came to the door to let me in. They were a very friendly and lovely couple who were glad to help in this match-making work. My date, Emil, was already there sitting in the living room with Mary and her husband. The first thing I noticed about him was his dark, wavy hair which reminded me of my first husband. His round, smooth face showed a much younger person than forty-six. He was neatly dressed in a dark grey suit, white shirt and grey striped necktie. When he stood up as Mary introduced him I also noticed that his height was about the same as my late husband's, about five feet and eight inches. I felt that he was attracted to me as much as I was to him.

Ica served coffee and cake and we talked about our life in Canada. After we left the house Emil walked me home and told me he would call. He did call the very next day. We dated mostly on weekends. He told me that he was very lonely and homesick in Canada and he was thinking of going back to Hungary. He also told me that he had been introduced to other women but that he didn't like them. "How about me?" I asked. "Do you like me even with a sixteen-year-old son?"

"Yes, I like you. Otherwise, I wouldn't have called you after our first date," Emil replied. We dated for about three months before we made plans to marry. I talked my plans over with my son who was very happy for me. He realized how hard it was for me to be alone. Andy understood that I had been burdened by the responsibility of trying to be both mother and father. I told Andy that I thought that my future husband was a good and wonderful man but that he was from a small village and that therefore he might have different interests from us who came from the capital city, Budapest. I asked my son always to treat his stepfather with respect.

My wedding and new job

Emil had a very good friend in Toronto who had arrived with his wife many years earlier than us. This friend of his sent the airplane ticket to him in Austria when Emil had written that he was there waiting for his turn to come to Canada. Emil took me to the home of this friend to introduce me and, I thought, to ask his opinion of me. His friend, Joe, told him to marry me before I changed my mind. The wedding took place on the 14th of December 1958 and Joe and his wife, Edith, organized and paid for it. We had a buffet-style wedding reception with plenty of food and sweets. There were about fifty people, all of them from Emil's side because I had only Aranka and her family on my side.

A lovely episode occurred on my wedding day. It was Sunday and the wedding was scheduled for two in the afternoon. In the morning I went to a Hungarian hairdresser nearby. Quite a few ladies were ahead of me. I didn't know any of these Hungarian ladies but most of them knew my future husband from home. One of the women said to the hairdresser, "Make a nice hairdo, Elizabeth, please, because today I'm invited to a wedding."

"Whose wedding are you invited to?" asked Elizabeth.

"I know only the groom who is Emil Grossman but I don't know the bride," was the answer. Overhearing the discussion I smiled to myself and said loudly, "Please, Elizabeth, make a nice hairdo for me too, because I'm the bride of Emil Grossman." Everyone laughed.

At my wedding I wore a royal blue suit and white silk blouse. I bought a white velvet hat with a short veil which covered half of my face. My fiancee gave me a bouquet of pale yellow and white flowers. Carrying the bouquet in my arms I slowly walked up to the canopy alone. Emil was there, already surrounded with his best friends, with the rabbi across from him waiting for my arrival. The ceremony was short but lovely. The rabbi, who was also Hungarian, gave a little speech about two lonely people in a foreign country who had found each other. He wished us all the best and asked us to keep the Jewish faith and to observe the Jewish traditions. Andy walked around with a camera taking pictures. We didn't have a professional photographer but Andy's pictures turned out very well.

We already had rented another apartment at the corner of Markham and College streets. It was a two-bedroom with another small room which we later rented to a young Hungarian man. We also had a kitchen, living room and a bathroom. Finally Andy had his own room and comfortable new continental bed. And, oh wonder of wonders, the following week Emil bought a television!

At that time Emil worked in a factory as a cabinet-maker. I still worked in the hospital but I hated my work there. First of all I started my job at six in the morning which meant that I had to get up a little before five a.m. Secondly, I thought that I was able to do more than cleaning washrooms. The factory where Emil worked was very far away from our apartment and every morning he got a ride with Hungarian friends. We started to talk about buying a used car. This would have been a luxury in Hungary and we had never been able to buy one there but in Canada it was a necessity.

One day I was called suddenly into the office at work and was told that my husband had had an accident and was in the Branson Hospital on Finch Avenue. "What happened to him? How badly hurt is he?" I forced the words out of my mouth feeling sick.

"He cut off two of his fingers with a saw," the clerk told me.

"I would like to go see him."

"He is probably sedated and wouldn't recognize you so it is no use to go." My boss didn't let me go but I went anyway without his permission. Emil was already out of the anaesthetic and was very glad to see me. He told me that the doctor wanted to amputate the thumb and index finger of his left hand.

He understood what the doctor wanted to do but all he could say, and he said it repeatedly, was "No! No!" This was useful and his fingers were saved. They were completely healed and usable but he was unable to work for about three months. After that he changed his job and went to another factory. That was the time to look for a car. After much looking and bargaining we finally bought a two-year-old Chevrolet. It was silvery blue with dark blue seats. It was a beauty and it was ours! I felt very rich owning a car. All of our friends came to see it and to inspect our new purchase. Emil took a few lessons and soon he learned to drive. I remembered how surprised I had been when I saw that the cleaning lady drove to her work in her own car in Winnipeg. "Look Andy," I had said to my son," here in Canada even the cleaning ladies own a car." Now that we had ours I understood its importance.

During this time I still attended English classes at night school and it finally paid off when I got a clerical job in the Bank of Montreal in April of 1961. We bought an English newspaper every day to be up-to-date with the news. One day I saw an advertisement for different jobs in the Bank of Montreal. I gathered all my courage and went to apply for a job with this bank. At that time there was an age limit for hiring staff. I was over the limit. For this reason they didn't want to hire me but I was very desperate to get out of my cleaning work in the hospital. In my desperation I started to cry. Then I remembered what I had read the previous evening. Still crying I said, "You don't want to hire me because my name is Grossman and I'm a Jew! Just last night I read in the paper that the banks don't want to hire Jews because they think after a while the Jews will want to own the banks." That was true at the time and when I had read it I thought first that I hadn't understood correctly. But my understanding was correct and the story was true. The management wanted to prove that it was not true.

"We already have Hebrew girls," said the person in charge. He didn't use the word Jew but Hebrew instead. I was hired. My job was in the coupons and bonds department and now I started work at nine o'clock in the morning!

One night a week we hired a sixteen-year-old Canadian student to teach us English. He was a busy young boy because he had many Hungarian pupils and he worked every night of the week. Sometimes instead of teaching us the language or its grammar he taught us by demonstrating how to make cheese burgers in the oven! He also told us stories about other Hungarian pupils that he had. Once he told us that he had a Hungarian lady student whom he called the "sausage lady." In answer to my question about why he had called her that the boy told us the following, "Mrs. M. has a young boy who behaved quite badly. Once she wanted to punish him but the boy ran away from her. His mother picked up a fifteen-inch-long sausage and chased him around the table with the sausage trying to hit him with it." We all laughed about the story and we still learned by listening to our young teacher.

I received three diplomas for my English studies. The first one was dated 21 March 1960 from the Toronto Board of Education, English and Citizenship School. Another diploma was from the Department of Education, Ontario, and the third one was from Central Technical School in May 1962.

Finally our big day to become Canadian citizens arrived. On 10 May 1962 my husband, son and I became Canadians. I was very happy! I had my family, my home, my work and my health in my new adopted country. Did I need more?

Elizabeth and her family come to Canada

Elizabeth's letters from Israel were still very desperate. In one of these she asked us if we could bring them to Canada. If we could lend them the money they would pay us back later. She wrote that she had asked Aranka first because she thought that Aranka and her family were in a better financial situation in Canada as they had been in Budapest but Aranka answered that they didn't have any money. After my husband read the letter I asked him, "What do you think about their problem? Would it be possible to help them?"

"Of course we'll help them. She is your sister." I kissed him for his generosity. We started to work on it and soon sent them the three airplane tickets.

They arrived on a bright sunny summer day in 1960. We were just ready to go to the airport for them when looking out the window I saw a limousine pull up to the front of our building. The had decided to take an earlier airplane and to surprise us with their arrival. As they got of the taxi I saw that Tomi was the one who had changed a lot. He was eight years old when I saw him last and now he was a much taller twelve-year-old. I ran down the steps to meet them calling out loudly to Emil, "They are here already!"

Emil also came down and after greeting them warmly he helped take their suitcases up to their room which was our tenant's before we sent him away to make room for my sister and her family. They stayed with us for three weeks and during that time we helped Frank to get a job in a factory as a cutter. We found an inexpensive apartment and after three weeks they moved out on their own. Elizabeth got a job in a hosiery factory. We introduced Elizabeth and her family to our friends and on weekends we took them everywhere we went, to beaches and on excursions.

When I changed from my cleaning job in the hospital to the bank Elizabeth took my place for a short time. One day as she was cleaning an Hungarian lady's room the patient started to converse with her in Hungarian. When my sister mentioned that the work was too heavy for her the lady replied, "I knew an Hungarian who also had worked here as a cleaning lady but after two years she became a clerk in the Bank of Montreal."

"Oh, I know that woman," Elizabeth replied, "she is my sister." We all laughed when Elizabeth told us about her conversation.

Tomi had no difficulty in school. He picked up the language fast and was an excellent student. He eventually became an architectural engineer. There was a police station close to the building where Tomi worked after he received his diploma. He often went there during his lunch break and made friends with some of the police. He liked their work so much that Tomi became a volunteer policeman. He still spends his free time doing it.

Andy graduated from Central Technical School but couldn't decide what career to choose. Finally he considered a career as a draughtsman. He entered a contract for a three-year apprenticeship to become a structural draughtsman. He worked at John T. Hepburn Ltd. Structural Steel Manufacturing and his work is now permanently encased in steel. He detailed the third and fourth floor of the famous Toronto-Dominion Centre in downtown Toronto.

I remember when the old Toronto Dominion Bank was being torn down on King Street across from the Bank of Montreal where I had worked. They were making way for the shiny new skyscraper that stands there today. We often watched the workers from our windows. I felt sorry for the pigeons who had their nests somewhere in the old building. They flew around like crazy when they couldn't find their nests when they started to demolish the building. It was the first high-rise bank building to be built in the mid-sixties and we watched it grow higher day by day in front of our eyes.

After not quite two years Andy wanted to discontinue his apprenticeship. He said he just couldn't stand those long hours in an office. However, I convinced him to finish his term so that he could get his diploma. After that he could decide what he wanted. He did what I asked him and after receiving his diploma he got a job at City Hall downtown and worked a few more years in his field.

Andy was crazy about cars and even while still in school he wanted very much to have one of his own. For a half a year he begged me to sign the paper so he could get his driver's license. He already knew how to drive because of his friends. Finally I signed the paper even though he was not yet seventeen. Now he wanted a car. He saved his money from working after school and he bought a used car for two hundred dollars. I will never be able to forget how happy he was when he held up his own car key. Andy was a careful and good driver.

One afternoon as I walked on Harbord Street I stepped off the sidewalk to cross the road and an old car appeared in front of me and almost hit me. I swore at the driver but I stopped immediately when I saw that it was my own son that I was wanting to send back to where he came from. Andy had seen me on the sidewalk and had deliberately driven in front of me.

During one summer holiday, Andy, and one of his best friends, David, went on a camping trip to Algonquin Park. He enjoyed it so much that he tried to persuade us to go also. He promised to lend us his tent and all the equipment we would need. He just wouldn't give up. So, finally Emil and I agreed and we started to prepare for a camping holiday. Friends of ours, a couple, asked if they could join us and share the expenses. Since the tent was big enough for all four and they were pleasant people, we agreed.

One Sunday morning we packed everything into our car and went to pick up our friends. Andy advised that we go to Algonquin Park which was about 220 miles away. I didn't even know that such camping places existed. Arriving there we could choose a place to our liking to set up the tent. We chose a place between huge pine trees where there was a picnic table and a barbecue stand. A little further off there were showers and toilets in a big building.

The two men set up the tent while Margit and I took out some meat and vegetables to prepare an early supper. By the time the tent was ready and the sleeping bags in place our cooking was also finished. We set the table with a plastic cover with printed red and yellow flowers on it and placed the paper plates, plastic cutlery, serviettes and cups. We were having a good time so far eating, talking, and laughing and we were glad we had come. There were a lot of young people with children. It was really a bargain holiday for a big family.

There was lots of wildlife. Among the trees, mostly pines, squirrels ran up and down on the trunks chasing each other playfully. We even saw a deer further back in the forest. The beach was still full of people playing ball or swimming and children were building sand castles. On our way back we picked strawberries which tasted so sweet that we just couldn't stop eating them. By the time we arrived at the tent it was dark. My husband lit the lamp and hung it in a tree above the table. It was so romantic. We talked and sang until bedtime. Then we took turns undressing in the tent and climbed into our sleeping bags. I was not a good sleeper and it was hard to fall asleep without reading in bed. It was especially hard because our friend, Mike, snored very loudly. In the morning I complained to him about it and he promised that he wouldn't snore the next night. I wondered how he could keep such a promise.

In the morning we sent the men out of the tent while Margit and I got dressed. She was a little taller than I but almost twice my size. Maybe she had just gained weight recently because everything was tight on her. Suddenly I heard a funny noise like someone ripping a piece of cloth. I looked at Margit, bent over with her back to me, and I saw that her slacks had ripped showing her behind. I started to laugh and she laughed with me so loud that the two men came running in to investigate what was happening.

The second night I was hoping for a peaceful and undisturbed sleep. This time Mike was indeed quiet but Margit started to snore. "Margit, are you snoring?" asked her husband.

"Yes," Margit replied in her sleep.

"Stop it or I'll throw you out," Mike threatened but Margit continued her sleeping and snoring and I didn't let Mike try to wake her up again. And that was the end of our camping. Our backs were aching from the hard ground and our sleep was disturbed so we decided to go to a motel to have a good rest. Despite the difficult nights those two days were fun.

My in-laws visit

My in-laws' letters from Hungary arrived every month and I answered them right away. Every year, on Mother's Day in May, my mother-in-law was the one who sent flowers for me. They paid for them in Budapest and the bouquet of flowers was sent from a Hungarian flower shop in Toronto.

When I wrote to them about my marriage they were terribly happy. In his letters papa started to hint how much they would like to see us and to know my new husband. Again I approached my husband. "Darling, would you agree to bring them over for a visit?"

"Yes, I would," Emil said without hesitation. In my next letter to Budapest I wrote that with Emil's approval we would start the necessary steps to bring them here for a visit. The answer to my letter was so moving that Emil had to turn aside to wipe away his tears. Papa wrote,

> You are the most generous two persons in the world. First you, my daughter, who always kept in contact with us not like many others who left their parents behind and very seldom or never wrote to them. And now your husband, who has nothing to do with us, who never saw or knew us, agreed to our coming over. We will appreciate this forever! We are the happiest couple in the whole city to know we will soon see our only grandson, the light of our eyes, and you, and to know our new son. Because Emil is going to be our son, instead of our own who we lost so young.

They had already applied to the Hungarian Government for a permit to come to Canada. We took some time from our work to go to the Immigration Office for their visa.

"What relationship are these persons to you?" asked the officer in charge.

"They are my late husband's parents," I told him.

"But you are married now. Is your present husband offering to bring over your first in-laws?" he asked.

"Yes, he agrees," I said.

"I have never experienced such a request before," the clerk said and added, "Your husband must be a very good human being." After we got the papers we needed we sent the two airplane tickets to them.

It was a cold, sunny spring day in March 1963 when we all went to the airport to meet my in-laws whom we hadn't seen for seven long years. Our tension grew when we heard that their airplane had arrived. Finally they were in front of us. Papa, still tall and slim in his early seventies and mama, small and somehow much more round than I remembered her. Mama's first words to Andy were, "My light of my eyes, you are not a little boy any more, you are a fine young man." It was true. Andy was now a very handsome twenty-one year old. After many hugs and kisses and some tears we took them home to our two-bedroom apartment on Clovely Street, just below Eglinton and west of Ossington.

They were very impressed with our 1958 silver-blue Chevrolet which was still in very good condition. They were equally impressed by our apartment which was in the top of a triplex. I gave them Andy's bedroom and Andy moved to the living room couch. When mama took off her coats she slimmed down. She had worn three coats and two of them were only a couple of their many presents; one for Andy and one for me.

All three members of my family had to go to work so my in-laws were on their own during the day. Mama did the cooking despite my opposition but she said that she had to have something to do. She even asked if Emil had any socks with holes in them that she could mend. I said laughingly that in Canada we don't mend socks if they have worn out but buy another pair. Together they took long walks hand-in-hand in the neighbourhood. One day they even walked north on Bathurst and stepped into a synagogue. They were surprised that no men had to wear skull caps (*yarmulke*). It was the Holy Blossom reform temple. On weekends we all went to the beach, to High Park, to Edwards Gardens and on other excursions. When we had some vacation time to spend with my in-laws Emil drove us to Montreal where they had old friends to see. I have some lovely, sometimes funny, memories about my in-laws during their five months visit in Canada.

Mama just loved to answer the telephone though she didn't have one at her home in Budapest and I don't think she could even phone from a booth. One night our telephone rang and again mama hurried to answer it. "May I talk to Andy?" a young girl asked in Hungarian.

"He can't come right now, my sweet child, because my grandson is in the bathtub washing his *tohesz*," she answered. She meant his behind.

One late spring in the early morning the whole family went to a farm where we had friends. We wanted to show it to my in-laws. First, we went to the chicken barn where we were shown the development of the chicken from the egg right up to the selling of the birds. In the huge barn there was an incubator on one side and under it we saw thousands of baby chickens. We could hardly get away from the tiny, fuzzy yellow chicks who were picking up seeds with their little beaks. On the other side of the barn were the big birds ready to be sold and shipped.

After lunch a young girl came over from the nearby dairy farm where she lived with her family. Emil happened to know the family from Hungary. The girl was introduced to us and Andy talked and joked with her. The seventeen-year-old girl, Magdi, asked if we would see her parents and show the farm to Andy's grandparents. We went over for a short visit and had a lovely time. I'll return to this young girl later in my story.

Mama always asked us the previous day what we would like for supper. One morning I took out a chicken from the freezer and asked mama to make breaded chicken. When I got home after work I found mama close to tears. "You made a mistake," she said. "The fowl you took from the freezer was not a chicken but a big hen and it was too old to make breaded chicken from it."

"But mama, it is a chicken even if it is so big," I comforted her. Finally I convinced her and together, in a hurry, we cooked the supper.

Another time, it was in May, I arrived home and stepped into the living room and was greeted by the sweet fragrance of my favourite flowers, lilac. There was a huge bouquet of them in the centre of the table. "Mama, where did you get the flowers?" I asked her.

"As papa and I were strolling along the sidewalk I saw a lady tending her garden," she said. "There was a beautiful bush with double dark lilacs on it. I know that lilac is your favourite so I wanted to have some for you."

"But how did you ask for them, mama? I know that you don't know any English," I said.

"It was easy," she answered. "I stopped, pointed to the tree and put my two palms together as if I were praying. The lady understood what I wanted and cut a bunch of the flowers for me."

"How did you thank her?"

"Oh, I just blew a kiss and smiled at her and she smiled back at me."

Mama repeated this procedure many times during their visit and I always had my favourite flowers in our home. My in-laws' most memorable outing was the one when we took them to Niagra Falls. All we Hungarians heard about Niagra Falls back in Hungary. We even had a song which praises this wonder of nature but we never imagined its beauty until we had seen the Falls. It had the same effect on mama and papa as it had had on us when we first saw the Falls. After papa took many pictures of the Falls we looked around the beauifully kept parks with colourful beds. Finally, we all sat down around a picnic table and Emil took out the picnic basket from the car. We had an unforgettable day together with our little family.

My in-laws' fiftieth wedding anniversary approached and we wanted to celebrate with a surprise party for them. We planned the party for a Sunday, a warm summer day in July. I prepared the food and ordered a big chocolate cake with the inscription "Happy Fiftieth Wedding Anniversary." I also ordered a magnificent flower centrepiece. It was three flower pots combined together. One was higher in the centre and two were lower on either side. Red roses in each of them were blown all over with gold dust. Three gold-coloured candles were in middle of each pot. We hid the centrepiece in the garage. I planned an early buffet-style supper. My sister, Aranka, and her husband lived only walking distance from us so I told them that I would send my in-laws over on that Sunday afternoon so I could set the table. When I told them to walk over to my sister's mama asked me, "Why do you want to get rid of us today?"

"I don't mama, but Aranka told me she would to have you over for an *espresso* coffee." They walked over. About five-thirty my family started to arrive. Elizabeth with her husband and son, Tomi, came as did Marianna and her husband. Finally, Aranka and her husband arrived with mama and papa. It was a family get-together which we very seldom had had before. They all brought presents, cards and flowers. After supper when they started to open the parcels my in-laws were very moved and tears of joy ran down their cheeks. Mama immediately changed her dress to a new light gray silk one that Emil and I had bought for her. It fit her perfectly. That is why in the pictures which Andy and Emil took turns taking mama was in two different dresses that night. That day was another memorable one among many with my in-laws during their visit.

Soon everything came to an end. The day came to say goodbye which was almost as emotional as the welcome when they first arrived. They needed an extra suitcase to take all the presents they received home. We all escorted them to the airport and we promised them that we would go back to Hungary to visit them. With this promise in their mind they took our farewell a little easier. After they left we went back to our old routines but we were still talking about them for a long time.

A visit to Israel

Our first big tour outside Canada with my husband was in 1965. Until this trip we had gone on smaller tours to

Montreal, Ottawa and also to the United State. But in 1965 we
went to Israel and on our way back we visited Paris for a few
days. While I was living in Hungary I never had the chance or
the money to see other countries. I was very excited to see
Israel where my husband's only brother and his family lived. I
can't describe the feeling when I first walked on the street of
the country where I had wanted to go with my little boy in
1949 when we were captured. I had a feeling that I was really
home because in Israel no one would hurt me for my Jewish-
ness. My brother-in-law laughed when I asked him, pointing
to a street sweeper, "Is he Jewish also?"

It was the first time that I met my brother-in-law Alex, his
wife Sarah and their eight-year-old son Avram. Alex had also
escaped from Hungary in 1949 and went to Israel in the same
year. The life there then was very hard. He settled down in a
small *moshav* where he got a tent and some money to live on.
He wanted to start farming and to do so he had to be married.
So, he married the first available woman he found. After the
marriage the government supplied them with materials to
build a small house which they had to do themselves and seeds
for grassland and a cow.

The two brothers were terribly happy to see each other after
many long years. They were well off when we arrived and
Alex wanted to pay all our expenses in the country. He bought
me a topaz ring in an eighteen-carat gold setting which I
treasure and have worn ever since. The village in which they
lived had a total population of roughly two hundred people,
all of whom were Hungarian. Alex introduced us to all his
neighbours. On one of our visits to a neighbour the host exclaimed when I told him my name, "Are you the one whose
fiance was Bela Boros?"

"Yes I am. What do you know about him?" I asked.

"I was Bela's and also your husband Zolti's comrade in the
concentration camp," he said. When he mentioned my late
husband's name I had a hard time not to show how emotional
it made me. Then he suddenly asked me, "Would you like to
meet Bela?" I looked at my husband who nodded.

"Yes," I said.

"Okay, I'll phone to tell him that you are here. He often comes to visit me," he said. "Come back tomorrow night," he added. It was a very unusual situation the next day when my present husband took me over to the man's house in a horse carriage to meet my former fiance. Bela looked a bit older, his pants needed ironing and his thick, wavy hair needed a cut. Around his big blue eyes were more tiny wrinkles when he smiled. We hugged each other and his first question was, "How is little Andy?"

"He is not so little any more, Bela. He is a young adult. And he is just fine." Then he wanted to see pictures of Andy which I showed him. Bela never remarried. I felt sorry for him. He looked so lonely but it was circumstance and fate which had pulled us apart. That was the last time ever that I saw my old fiance. Some years later another comrade of my first husband, who also had lived in Israel since 1949 with his family, wrote to me about Bela. He had been their frequent visitor and he adored their children. Bela had been on his way to see them with a couple of chocolate bars in his shirt pocket for the children. But before he reached them he suffered a heart attack. He was fifty years old when he died.

Back to Hungary

For more than ten years even the thought of going back to Hungary made me very uncomfortable. In the first few years in Canada I had recurring nightmares in which I returned to Hungary and then was not allowed to return to Canada. I would wake up perspiring and sometimes in tears and was awfully happy that it had only been a dream. But after almost twelve years of my in-laws' repeated requests I decided to go back to see them. In the summer of 1968 both Emil and I travelled to Budapest.

We arrived on a warm summer day and we took a taxi to Nepszinhaz Street 16. That was the apartment building where we had lived together for some short years with my Zolti and, after his death, with his parents. That was the house to which I had brought my new baby home to and the house from which we had been taken. That was our home where I slept fully dressed during the night in case the gendarmes came for us. This was the house where I hurried back in the hour of our liberation, to beg some food for papa who was dying from hunger. From this house I escaped in 1949 only to be captured and again, with success in November 1956.

And now, in 1968, I stood in the same yard looking around before I entered the kitchen of our apartment. Now there are weeds growing between the red stones in the courtyard and the whole building is kept from collapsing by many huge beams.

Finally I stepped into the kitchen with Emil behind me. Mama was at the stove cooking supper for us. She looked up as she heard the door oppen and with a cry, "You are here!" she ran the few steps to us with outstretched arms. We held each other crying. Papa, hearing that we had arrived came out from his room. He too hugged and kissed us and I saw tears welling behind his eyeglasses. They were much older by now and papa wasn't feeling well. Seeing his long, white hair, the gathering tears in his eyes, his much heavier body caused by his liver ailment, memories rushed again into my mind. Was he the same man who once, a long time ago, wanted to report me to the authorities for my escape from the country? Now I felt sorrow and love toward him. I wanted to be with him and mama as much as I could in those short three weeks that we had together.

Mama loved to go to a market which was only a few blocks away to get everything fresh in the morning. I went with her many times. I even took a photograph of her holding a live duck which she had just bought. She wanted to cook me a favourite dish, long since untasted, of roast duck and liver. The first few days neighbours from the building who knew me from before came to see me and my new husband. Mama proudly introduced him, "He is Ibi's husband, my Emil." She loved him very much.

During our visit we also went to Emil's hometown. When we arrived in this small village, where everyone knew him and his family, he was welcomed as if he were a brother to everyone. We stayed a couple of days at this old neighbour's house. It was very moving to see how the whole village came to see him and invited us to their home. In my entire life I haven't drunk as much wine as in those two days. In every home we were offered a glass of wine. I didn't want to be impolite so I sipped a little at everyone's place who had invited us. Of course I was happy and laughing from all this sipping and people said to Emil, how nice and merry his wife is.

We also went to Lake Balaton with a cousin of mine who had a cottage there. This cousin, Joe Fabian, was from my mother's side of the family. He also had lost his family and had a second wife and two children after the war. The three weeks went by very fast. We had to return to our work. The boss of the butcher shop where Emil then worked would barely let him take even three weeks. He was a very good and conscientious worker who not only his boss but also the customers missed very much.

It is always worst for those who stay behind. Seeing mama and papa standing at the front of the house, waving goodbye as we left for the airport in a taxi, was very sad. I promised to visit them again soon.

Andy's marriage and my first grandchild

It was in that same year that Andy met a girl. Andy worked in Toronto City Hall as a draughtsman. One day he went to the bank in the same building. The teller, a young girl, asked him, "Don't you remember me?" Andy looked at her.

"No," he replied.

"You were at our farm with your parents and grandparents some years ago," the girl said.

"Oh yes! I remember now. Your name is ..."

"Magdi," answered the young girl, helping him to remember. "You know, " she continued, "I always wished that some day your parents would bring you to our farm again, but they never did."

"Now here I am," Andy said, "and if you are free on Saturday night your wish will be granted and we could get together again." They dated for a while and one day in the early fall Andy announced to us that he had proposed to her. The next Sunday we all went to Magdi's parents place to celebrate the engagement. Both sides were satisfied with their child's choice. The wedding took place on 14 December 1968 in Hamilton. The same day was Emil's and my tenth wedding anniversary. Magdi is a lovely, family-oriented girl. She loved her parents and her only sister, Margaret. She also seemed to be happy to have another mother and father as she called us after the wedding. We had a good relationship, not like mother and daughter-in-law, but like mother and daughter.

Andy had never really like his profession and he was unhappy in his work. He always wanted to do something which would be on his own. After much thinking and discussing between myself and my husband we decided to help him financially to buy a taxi. Andy had his own business now and he made a living driving his taxi. Later we helped him buy another one which he rented to a driver.

Two years after their marriage Magdi became pregnant. On a gorgeous day, Sunday 23 May 1971, we were invited to our friends for a barbecue. Magdi was expecting her baby any day so I told Andy where to reach us just in case. We had just started to eat when the phone rang. In a couple of minutes my girlfriend came out and said that the call was for me. Somehow I knew that it was good news. "Hello, mother, congratulations! You have just become a grandmother." I heard my son's voice on the other end.

"Oh, I am so happy! What is it, a boy or a girl? Is the baby all right? And how is Magdi?" I asked him excitedly, not waiting for any answers.

"Calm down, mother! They are okay. It is a girl. No, he is a boy," my son teased me.

"Make up your mind, Andy, and tell me already, what is it?" I told him laughing.

"Seriously, mother, he is a boy as I ordered him to be. His

name is David," my son said finally. I was very happy for my first grandchild but still a little bit confused too. Am I an old lady now, I wondered? All the grandmothers were old and white-haired when I was a child. We excused ourselves from our friends and left for the hospital to visit our daughter-in-law and the baby. The baby was a perfect little thing. After the first three months he spent many weekends with us. He was very easy to care for, a very good-natured baby. In his first years he was tiny for his age but very advanced in other ways. At the age of ten months he had already started to walk and a month later he said his first words.

In that year, 1971, a sad event also happened. My sister's husband, Jeno, died suddenly of a heart attack. He was sixty-two years old. My husband and I were away in New York visiting Emil's sick cousin when it happened. We had only enough time for a weekend visit but the day after our arrival the phone rang. "It is Andy from Canada," said my husband's cousin. I got very scared because I suspected something bad had happened.

"Andy, what is wrong?" I asked my son with palpitating heart.

"Mother, Jeno has died"

"What Jeno?" It didn't reach me that there was only one Jeno in the family.

"Your brother-in-law. The funeral is to take place tomorrow, Sunday afternoon."

"We're coming back as soon as we can get on an airplane, Andy." Next day, when we arrived home, we had just enough time to get to the funeral. Aranka was devastated. As the years passed she became more and more bitter and lonely. I associated with her and understood her feelings because I went through the same loneliness. Bus she said that in my case it was different because I was young and still had some hope for the future. She was right.

My brother-in-law had adored my seven-months-old grandson. The would have been very good friends just as he had been with my son. I remember a visit to my sister and her family when Andy, then four years old, jumped up and down on their couch a few times. When Aranka ordered him to stop and get down the little boy said, "I can do anything I want because uncle Jeno and I are friends. Isn't it so Jeno?" "That is true, Andy. You just continue to jump." Jeno had worked in the Toronto Harbour Commission as a sort of financial advisor. He was loved by every one equally, colleagues and management. When my sister was called into the office to arrange the pension for her, the manager told her that their loss was also great because Jeno's work was almost irreplaceable.

My in-laws' illness

I still wrote letters diligently to my in-laws every month and papa always answered immediately. His writing was even and small like tiny pearls. When he became sick it showed in his letters which started to appear much larger and uneven. One day early in 1973 we received a letter from mama's nephew, Jeno. He wrote that the remaining nephews and nieces of mama would like to celebrate their aunt and uncle's sixtieth wedding anniversary. Mama had had eleven sisters and brothers but only three of them lived through the Holocaust. But she had quite a few nephews and nieces. Jeno also wrote that papa was very sick with terminal cancer and did not want this celebration. Still, the relatives had decided to go ahead and they invited us to this anniversary.

Emil and I decided to go to Hungary to see them. This time it was a very sad meeting. Papa was in bed all the time, too weak to get up. I sat at his bedside holding his hand or stroking his face and forehead. He smiled at me and said in a low voice, "You are a good woman. You always have been good to us. God bless you." Emil and I, with his other relatives, were at his bedside when the rabbi remarried them on their sixtieth wedding anniversary. We made a toast to papa's health and he took a little of his wedding cake from my hand. I was glad to have been there that summer of 1973 because in a couple of months papa died.

After his death mama took in her nephew Jeno and his wife, Irma. They hadn't had an apartment and by taking them into hers mama was ensuring that it would automatically go to them after her death. Mama couldn't cope with the departure of her husband of sixty years. She also became sick and Irma took good care of her. Then, one day, we received a letter from Irma saying that if we wanted to see mama alive we had better travel to Hungary. It was Christmas, 1974. This time I travelled with my son.

When she saw her only grandchild after so many years mama cried hard and told him repeatedly, "You are here, my light of my eyes. You are here." During the two weeks visit I stayed with mama most of the time but she sent her grandson out to have some fun. When Andy and I took her outside for a short walk she was so weak we had to support her on both sides. A few months later when I received the telegram my heart started to beat very loudly. It came from Budapest and the news in it couldn't be about anyone else but mama. I was right. Opening it I saw a few words, "Your mother-in-law died peacefully Yesterday. Irma." I sat down with the telegram and my thoughts went far back to mama. I married her only son when I was very young and she was like a second mother to me.

Mama was the one who took me to the hospital when my child was due to be born. When my son was four months old I had to say goodbye to my husband who was taken to labour camp. When we were clinging to each other, crying, mama was the one who gently separated us. He was her son but she wanted to be strong for our sake. We were together on an open field when the gendarmes selected the young ones to go to the concentration camp. Mama was the one who went to a policeman whom she knew from her hometown to beg for my life. In the ghetto mama almost starved to death because the few little buns she made from the last grams of flour and water she saved for us. After our survival when we learned the terrible news about my husband's death mama comforted me though her loss was also great. In 1949 when I decided to escape from my country with my child only mama knew about it and, holding her tears, she escorted us to the train. After we were caught and put in jail she came to that strange city to take her grandson home. The telegram said she was gone. A piece of my life was gone with her. Our little grandson gave us so much pleasure. David, as a baby and later as a small boy, was very good-natured. I have many fond memories of him. He loved music, even as a tiny baby. I bought some children's records which he liked to listen to, sitting on the stool that his grandfather had made him. The stool was approximately 12 inches long and seven inches high and eight inches wide. My husband painted it with a colour which looked like natural wood. The record player sat on a chair and David would watch the record going around as he sat on his little stool in front of the chair. He had a favourite song that he listened to repeatedly. Its title was "The Little Red Caboose." The song's story is about a train which carries children to a camp but which couldn't climb to the top of a mountain. The little red caboose is at the end of the train and it tries to push them up three or four times, but the train slides back. Finally, on the fifth try, the train gets up to the top of the mountain. I knew my grandson would cry out to me, as he did every time he listened to that record, "Mama, he made it!"

David had a little suitcase in which he carried his belongings whenever he stayed overnight. Once, after a weekend with us, it was time for him to go home. "Pack your things, David. It is time to go," I said to him. He did as I said and I watched him from the corner of my eye as he struggled to pull the zipper around the bag.

Noticing that I was watching him he stopped, looked up, and said, "This is very hard work for you, mama. It is only for men like papa and me." He was three years old.

On another occasion he decided to get rid of his old toys. He came up with the idea of having a garage sale. I made a sign, "Garage Sale," and he took out some of his toys and put them on the front lawn. Sitting on his tool beside his sign he waited for customers to come. Some people from the neighbourhood saw the sign and came over to ask what was for sale. I had told him beforehand that he should ask 25 cents per piece and he had agreed. Watching him I saw that the only customer he had he gave two toys for the price of one. I didn't interfere in his business but at the end of the sale I asked, "Why did you give two toys for 25 cents instead of one?"

"Because 25 cents is a lot of money. But look mama, I also got two candies, so that was really a good deal." To me it was obvious that he had no business sense yet but he certainly had a good heart! He was then only four years old.

Whenever we took him for a ride he was very observant and everything interested him. Once he saw a long train moving slowly and he cried out happily, "How lucky I am to see a train! Did you see it too, mama?" He asked me hoping I would be able to share in his happiness.

David was six years old when his mother told him that next day she would know if she was having another baby. David was very excited and could hardly wait for the next day. After his mother had informed him that the results were positive and he was going to have a baby brother or sister he jumped on his bike and drove around the neighbourhood yelling, "I'm going to have a baby!"

My second grandchild

One morning, a cold day in February 1978, I got up earlier than usual. It was a Sunday and I didn't have to go to work. Stepping into the kitchen I saw a piece of white paper on the table. Curiously, I picked it up. It was in my son's handwriting.

Here is Kati!! Born 3:10 a.m. today. She is eight and one half pounds. Her hair is black, her eyes blue, and she has chubby cheeks.

My son and daughter-in-law kept the baby's arrival a secret so as not to worry me. Kati was an adorable baby but quite different in nature from David. For the first three months of her life she cried constantly. We couldn't have her in our home as often as her brother because Kati would not stay. She couldn't sleep anywhere else but in her own crib. But occasionally she stayed, sometimes for days when she got older, and her parents were away. As the baby grew and started to talk she called me mama just as she heard David do. At home both children were quite messy. In our home no toys were brought into the living and dining rooms. They had their own room in our house so they could play there.

When Kati was about two years old she and her brother came to stay with us for a few days. One day during her visit I had lain down on the living room couch to rest. Kati may have thought that I was sleeping so she carried the small stool, which she had inherited from David, into the living room. I raised my head to investigate the groaning and dragging noises she made as she did this. When Kati saw that I was not sleeping she stopped and said loudly, "Back." She turned and carried the stool out of the living room. Her long curly hair was bouncing on her shoulders as she walked with her still unbalanced baby steps.

On another occasion, when Kati was about three years old, she changed her dress all by herself in her room in our home and threw it, turned inside out, on a chair. I had just stepped into her room in time to hear her saying to herself, "Mama wouldn't like this!" She then picked up her dress, reversed it from inside out, folded it neatly and placed it on the chair.

"That's my baby," I said hugging and kissing her.

The year in which Kati was born was the year in which I decided on an early retirement from the bank where I worked. The staff threw a very lovely party for me. It was held at the assistant manager's house about ten days prior to my last day of work. Every one was invited from the office with their spouses or dates. I was the centre of attention and felt like a bride at a bridal shower. I received a dozen crystal wine-glasses from colleagues.

Dereck, our young Irish manager, contrived an interesting game beforehand. Half of the staff wrote a sentence, any sentence, on a piece of paper. The other half each wrote a question. Then randomly one read the question and another answered with one of the written answers. During the game Dereck teased me about an occasion when I had gone to work on a holiday, 11 November, and then was left wondering why nobody else had shown up for work!

On my last day at work the girls sent me out of the office with some excuse. While I was gone they put a bouquet of red roses, a cheque and a huge card on my desk. I was very moved by this and went to every one of them to thank them for it with a hug. Dereck, my office manager, let me go home earlier than usual. My thank you card to the staff read,

Dear everybody,

While I write these few lines the roses are in front of me, so is the card with all twelve of your lovely writings, which I have read over and over.

I managed to smile during my farewell but as soon as I was out of the office and the door was closed behind me I started to cry. Seventeen years is a very long time and I felt that I was saying goodbye to a part of my family. What Dereck wrote to me is very true therefore I would like to quote it here.

"Ibi, they say a woman's work is never done. This is why women can enjoy retirement so well because they must keep active or they get bored. You can now put aside the daily chore of coming to work, remember the good times, and make your future fun by doing the things you did not have time for before."

Yes, Dereck, I will keep myself busy, I have more time for my family now, I try to keep my health, and I certainly don't feel old at sixty. Thank you again for the lovely going away party, for the beautiful gifts and for the surprise bouquet, card and cheque.

Today is Monday morning, my first weekday at home and I can't help but tell you the dream I had last night. I was in the bank looking for a job. A lot of girls lined up in front of me. Finally I got a job too and I wanted to get into the elevator to go to the appointed floor but I couldn't reach any of them, no matter how fast I ran. At each one the door closed before I could step in. Was it symbolic of my fear of elevators? Did it also mean that the years had passed by so fast and I was sorry not to be in the productive work force any more? Whatever it meant it was a funny dream.

Thanks again for everything. God bless you all.

Love, Ibi.

And with this another chapter of my life closed.

After my retirement I was still called back to work for a couple of months every year. November was the busiest month of the year and they needed my help when saving bonds went on sale. But after about three years the bank no longer allowed outside help.

I joined a seniors group which was close to our home and I tried to occupy my self with many things including painting once a week, needlework, crochet and folk dancing. I also joined a creative writing group and did some volunteer work weekly in the Sick Children's Hospital. I liked being with children but it was quite different with sick children. The play room where I worked every Monday was bright and cheerful.

The morning sun came through two huge windows. As soon as I entered the room I put the children's favourite record on the record player and then took the toys from the cupboard. I spread them on the small tables. After I put the "Open" sign on the door at nine o'clock the nurses started to bring the children in. Some of them were in wheelchairs or beds and those who could walk just came without any aids. My boss, a young woman, was usually on the ward by that time visiting the children, checking to see whether any of them needed toys in their room, and whether they were allowed to come to the play room.

Almost every week I could see different faces. Only a few of them stayed longer. The ward where I worked was the orthopaedic surgery ward. Fortunately, the parents were allowed to be with their children any time of the day. However, some children were from out of town or their parents were working and they could see them only at night or weekends.

One day I saw an Italian woman. She didn't look young enough to have a five-year-old son. The boy was strapped to the wheelchair. He couldn't speak or understand anything and he couldn't even hold himself in his chair. My heart went out to the mother who was with him all the time and talked to him as if he were a normal child. Maybe some day she would get some results with her patience, kindness and love for her child.

Sometimes we had so many children in the play room that I had to ask the nurses to take some of them back to their room because there were too many to handle. I knew I couldn't show any of my feelings but it was hard not to. One morning a new little girl was wheeled in, lying on her tummy in her crib. Her long, curly blond hair spread on her back and her chubby hands clasped the sides of the crib. She was motionless and as I went over to stroke her hair she startled at my unexpected touch. I spoke gentle, soothing words to her, patting her back. She was awake but didn't open her eyes. Soon her parents came with a beautiful bouquet of flowers and put it beside her head. When I stepped back to another child a nurse told me that the little girl with the cherubic face was blind. She couldn't see the wonderful bouquet her parents had brought her.

I went out to the corridor so that no one would see my tears. While there I heard a baby crying in her room so I went to see her. The tiny, maybe six-month-old child was crying her heart out. There was a bottle beside her but it was out of her reach. It was against the regulations to pick up any baby but I couldn't help but take the tiny thing out of her crib and cradle her in my arms. She stopped crying, only too happy to be picked up. She looked at me and smiled with tears still in the corners of her eyes. As I rocked her back and forth she fell asleep and I gently put her back in her crib. I went back to the play room with both of our tears dry, mine and the baby's.

During my outing the nurses had brought a girl and her brother in. A few days before they had been hit by a car as they crossed the street with their grandmother. The children were only four and five years old. They were in bad shape but thank God, they were getting better, and neither of them was going to be crippled.

On that day the hand of the clock on the wall slowly went to twelve and we had to take the children back to their rooms for lunch. I put away the toys, tidied up the room and closed the door behind me. Out in the beautiful, sunny street I tried to forget all those miseries but I just kept thinking of them for a long while. As I walked to the subway I recalled another children's hospital back in Budapest whose rules had given me a sleepless night.

One day in Budapest, when I went home from work, I found my forever active son lying motionless on the sofa. When I bent to kiss him I discovered that he was burning with fever. "How long has this been going on?" I asked my frightened mother-in-law.

"An hour ago he was still out in the yard playing, then he came in complaining about a headache and lay down," she replied. I called the family doctor, telling his secretary that it was an emergency. He came soon and roughly examining the child said he suspected a dreadful illness, meningitis. The doctor called an ambulance and we took my son to the children's hospital. There was rule in the hospital that visiting hours were restricted to certain days. I didn't understand how they could have such regulations. A sick child in a strange environment, not seeing his mother or someone close to him, must have experienced an awful time. I had to leave my child there and I went home wondering how I would make it through the night. In front of my eyes I could see my only child fighting for his life.

By the next morning I was half out of my mind not knowing what had happened to my son. It wasn't a visiting day but I made up my mind to see him. I went to the hospital and sneaked up to his room. All I wanted was to see him at the door. Slowly, I opened the door and peeped into the room. There were about ten cribs and all the children were lying in them except one. When I looked into the room I was expecting to see the same almost lifeless child I had left behind the previous day. One little boy was sitting in his crib with a pair of earphones over his ears. He must have sensed my presence because he looked up and saw me in doorway. "Mommy, mommy I am listening to the sleeping beauty on the radio!" His voice was the nicest music I ever heard.

Back in Budapest with David, 1983

With my in-laws gone I thought I would never go back to Hungary. While they were alive I felt an obligation to visit them. In 1983 my grandson, David, hinted at a wish. He very much wanted to go to Hungary to see the country where his parents and grandparents had originated. And here I was thinking to fulfil my grandson's wish and go back home with him. Did I say home? No! My home is here in Canada, the country that took us in, gave us work and a new life. But then why did I still call Hungary "home?" I think maybe because, despite what had happened, I was born and raised there. I didn't know any language other than Hungarian. As much as I wanted to forget that I was Hungarian I couldn't just as I couldn't forget our sufferings and the killings. In the ghetto, with David's father a baby, we were so many times so close to death. I had only one goal in front of me; to live! I never dreamed that some day I would be able to go abroad and return with my grandson!

As David's twelfth birthday approached his grandfather and I decided to take him to Hungary as a birthday present. He was very happy! However, I had two requests for him. First, he had to write a diary daily while in Hungary; secondly, he had to learn more of the language. David already understood quite a lot but he spoke only a few words. His birthday was in May but we had to wait until the end of the school year. The trip was scheduled for the first half of July. During the three intervening months David improved his Hungarian very much.

Finally the day came for our departure. David was very excited. This was his first trip outside his country of birth and also his first trip by airplane. It was a long journey. At the airport in Hungary, Irma and her boyfriend (her husband had died some years before), were waiting for us. When I wrote to tell them that we would be visiting Hungary Irma offered her apartment which she had inherited from my in-laws, the same apartment Andy and I had lived in before we escaped.

I thanked her and accepted her offer because I knew that the apartment was nice and cool during hot summers. That year was especially hot. I was glad that we would be staying in my old home even if it wasn't very comfortable. At least it would be cool.

As soon as we got off the plane at the Budapest airport we went to a waiting room where I saw Irma among the crowd because she is a tall woman. She is not related to us by blood but she was better to us than any close relative. She received us with open arms and hearts. If for nothing else, I loved her because she was very good to mama when she was terribly sick. We arrived about four o'clock in the afternoon. David was so tired that when we got home he went to bed and slept through the next day to noon. After his long sleep he was very much alert and hungry.

We tried to take David to as many places as we could.

Budapest was full of tourists, not only from the surrounding countries, but from as far away as Australia ad America. Because of this we couldn't get as many reservations as we wanted for places to see. For a few days we visited the village where Emil had lived. For a city boy everything was interesting and exciting in the small Hungarian village: the pigs in the pigpen, the pigeons on the roof and the chickens in the yard. Dogs and cats were running about freely. David was fascinated at how the cows knew their homes when they came back from pasture every afternoon.

In the family we stayed with there were two girls; one was five and the other was nine. The nine-year-old, Vicki, showed David everything. They fed the pigs and chickens together. Most of the children in the village wanted to see the little foreigner from Canada. With some of them they exchanged little souvenirs. Once, when we were invited to visit a family, the host said to David, "You are as lovely as a girl!"

David, who understood the man's words, got very angry and answered in Hungarian, "Get out!" pointing at the door. Everybody laughed and they thought it was rather cute, David sending the host out of his own home.

While we were in that village Vicki's parents, who had a car, took us to a very interesting place. It was a famous tourist attraction. It was a four mile long stalactite cave in a town called Agtelek. The cave was very cold and dark. There were some light bulbs hanging from the ceiling to give just enough light to see where we were stepping. The stone formed different shapes and icy water dripped down the walls. A guide led us through from the entrance to the exit at the other end.

Back in Budapest we took David to the famous Hungarian circus, to the zoo, and to sightsee around the city with an English-speaking guide. We went to the same outdoor swimming pool, Palatinus, where his daddy as a child rang the bell for the artificial waves. We also went to the indoor swimming pool where my son was trained for the Olympics before we escaped. I showed David his daddy's school and the nearby playground where he played football with his friends. I managed to get a ticket on a tour bus to go around Lake Balaton.

People called it the Hungarian Ocean. The best fish came from there. The water is warm and you can wade for miles before it gets deep. Also, the whole region is famous for its grapes and wines.

We had our lunch in a lovely restaurant where the tables were set in a garden full of geraniums and other flowers. Two gypsies played the violin during our lunch and with our meal we sipped *Badacsonyi*, one of the best wines of Hungary. The wine made me happy and I laughed continuously and called David by my son's name, *Andris*. David smilingly asked me, "Are you tipsy, mama? I'm your grandson, David, not *Andris*." He had to remind me a few more times of his name. But I didn't think that it was only the wine which made me say my son's name to my grandson. It was the fact that Andy was almost the same age as David when we lived in Budapest before we left the country.

On our way back our tour guide asked the passengers, who were from sixteen different countries, to sing a song from their country. David was very shy at first when the guide asked him to represent Canada with his song. Finally he did and after he finished he started to sing Hebrew songs as well. We were pleasantly surprised when some of the passengers joined him in the Hebrew songs.

During the summer the theatres and operahouses were closed in Budapest. But there are a few outdoor theatres where there were musical plays. We were lucky to get tickets to a well-known Hungarian musical called *Ecseri Wedding*. David enjoyed it tremendously and when it was finished he wanted to stay to see it again but this was not possible.

On another outing we went to a ceramic museum to see the works of a famous sculptor, Margit Kovacs. The museum was in Saint Endre, which is a small half-island on the river Danube, about a one-hour train ride from Budapest. The whole city, with its cobblestones, narrow streets and tiny houses, reminded me of my birthplace, Pécs. As I was walking in the unknown but still familiar streets for a while I forgot who and where I was. I was a little girl again, hopping from stone to stone, looking through the low windows of the little houses. On the next corner, if I turned right, or maybe left, I would step into father's small tinsmith shop. I stopped for a second to decide which way to turn when my grandson interrupted my thoughts, "Which way to go, mama?" Suddenly I came back from the past. I hugged my darling and said, "Just straight ahead, *eletem*." That is the term I used with him many times, it means "my life" in English.

We visited the charming Margaret Island, the picturesque Fisher-Bastion, and the gracefully built parliament buildings. We also took David to the 150-year-old Jewish synagogue which was the centre of the ghetto in 1944. Now it is an attraction for the many tourists that come from around the world. There are still services held in the old synagogue and we all went to a Saturday morning service.

One day, as we were strolling on Elizabeth Boulevard, David noticed a window in a small shop which caught his attention. In the window there were all kinds of miniature stuffed animals. He just couldn't leave the window so we stepped into the shop to buy some of them. After he chose seven or eight of those adorable tiny animals I told David that that was enough. When he reached number fifteen, I said firmly, "It is enough!" He chose two more, to the delight of the saleslady, who was smiling through all of David's shopping. He still treasures his little zoo. No matter how much my grandson enjoyed his trip at the end of the three weeks he counted not only the days but the hours until he would be arriving back home. He kept his promises and wrote his diary every night before he went to bed. He could also converse in Hungarian with people in Hungary.

Barmitzvah

Another year passed by and another big event came up in our family, David's barmitzvah.

On 16 June, a Saturday morning in 1984, a handsome boy, with greenish-blue eyes and light brown wavy hair, stood on the pulpit. His cheeks were smooth and peach-coloured with excitement. David courageously and charmingly recited his part from the Holy Book, the Torah. As I admired him I just couldn't believe that time had passed so fast and my baby grandson had become a man according to the Jewish law. Tears of joy were pouring down my face as I listened to my son's speech.

> Today you are barmitzvah! A son of the Covenant, a man in the eyes of God and your peers. We are here to celebrate a joyous occasion and an age old tradition. We have our relatives and friends with us to share our *simcha*. But it is important that while we celebrate our happiness today, we should remember those who can't be here, especially your two grandfathers. But such is life and they are gone. Instead we have our beloved papa who loves us the same way as our real father would.
>
> In the cemetery in Hungary stands a monument marking the final resting place of some of the six million martyrs of the Holocaust, my father, your grandfather, among them. On this monument there is an inscription; "Hatred has killed them / May love cherish their memory." You, my son, represent that love. You *are* that love! You are a link in a chain that was nearly broken, but was not! And you are here as living proof of the miracle of life, of Judaism and of Tradition.

How right my son, Andy, was with his speech! Because of sickness and hunger his life was like a decreased, flickering candle. It was a miracle that he stayed alive. And now his life continues in his son and the chain which was almost broken is not.

In another part of his speech he said,

> Your barmitzvah cake is in the form of a book, your mother and I chose it to symbolize your life ahead of you. You are going to get out of it what you put into it. This book is open, you are going to write its chapters, but the most important treasures are your heart and your head which are within you. My grandfather taught me that what is inside a person's head nobody can take from him. You have often heard from me that

if I teach you only one thing, how to think for yourself and use your own head, then I have done a good job as a father.

Those were also true words, my son. You said it very nicely to your son. Your grandfather would have been very proud of you. David's speech was also lovely. He thanked his parents, grandparents and relatives for the love and help they gave. Of course he mentioned his little sister Kati, who was six years old and who gave him much trouble when he baby-sat her. "But I love you anyway," he said. "I wouldn't trade you for anything (except maybe my own television)." In his speech, mentioning us, he said, "Mama and papa, I have spent much time with you since I was little and stayed at your home on many weekends. The little trips and adventures we have been on together, teaching me along the way a different perspective on life, that has enabled me to appreciate the kind of life I have here." David looked at us and said, "I thank you."

"I am happy, *eletem*, that you learned from us to value your life here," I answered him silently.

In early autumn of the same year the Festival of Festivals was celebrated and old movies were shown in cinemas and also in some parks. It was a hot summer day despite the fact that it was already September. My grandson spent many Fridays with us and slept overnight in our place. That special Friday night there was an entertainment and film in Earl Bales Park which is about fifteen minutes from our house. It is a very popular place for people who come from all over the city for a picnic, celebrations, or a stroll. During the summer old folks played cards all day long.

I wanted to see the programme and movie on that night and I asked my grandson if he would like to come. "I would rather watch T.V., mama," he replied.

"You can watch T.V. any other time but this Festival is only once a year," I tried to convince him. Finally he agreed to come. I took a blanket and a sweater for each of us in case the weather cooled off. Before we even reached the park we heard the music and saw the lights and balloons and big crowd. It was already almost dark but not yet dark enough for the movie. As we approached the huge screen a couple of young girls offered popcorn free. "Here, take a bag," she told David, "and there is a bag for your mother."

"My mother!" exclaimed my grandson but he took the bag of popcorn handed to me and with a kiss on my cheek said, "That was a compliment, mama."

"It is half dark so the girl couldn't see me well," I replied. But my grandson, who is such a little gentleman as he has always been from childhood, said firmly, "It is not that dark yet."

"Okay, it is too bad that she didn't say it in the morning so I would have a good day all day long." We spread the blanket not far from the screen and watched the dancers who already started their programmes. They were from different countries and the dances reflected their nationalities. To my surprise David said that he was sorry not to have come earlier.

When the movie started we moved further back to get a better view. The movie was interesting and entertaining for children and adults equally. It was a gangster film set in the twenties, "Bugsy Malone." The difference with other gangster films was that children acted the parts. They used eggs and foam in their guns instead of bullets. Since they were under age they pedalled old-fashioned automobiles. There were two groups of gangsters fighting for power. There was love in it and romantic scenes and also funny situations. We heard laughter mostly from the children in the audience.

The weather was still warm when it was finished close to 11 p.m. and the crowd started to leave. It was an unusual sight to see all those people, many of them carrying lawn chairs, walking in groups at that late hour. The spirit was high, people were laughing and talking about the night's entertainment. I was glad that David had had a good time and we walked home arm in arm talking quietly all the way. It was beautiful to be with my grandson, who at the age of thirteen was not ashamed to go out with his grandma and even to kiss her in front of other people. Probably David will soon forget the whole episode but I will always treasure that night with my grandson.

It was a summer morning in 1987 when my phone rang. An unfamiliar voice said, "Aunt Ibi, its me, Susie Shenker. I'm here from Budapest for a visit." I was surprised and glad as well to hear this young woman's voice. Susie was born after the war but her older brother was a good friend of my son. They lived and still live in the same apartment building where we lived before we left the country. Susie's mother and brother and my son and I went through a lot of terrible times during the war. Now Susie informed me that she had arrived with her sixteen-year-old daughter and ten-year-old son to visit a close friend of hers.

The next day my husband I went to fetch them from her friend's house. I spent much time with her and her children and took them to visit many places. They were very much impressed by our Canadian lifestyle. Susie especially liked how the senior citizens were treated here. I told her about the many ethnic senior clubs and homes, the activities they are able to do and the privileges they receive from government.

Once I happened to take them to the Eaton's Centre on seniors' day. There were programmes by seniors and Susie wanted to see as much of them as was possible. We stopped at the front of a group of senior dancers. They all wore white slacks, white blouses with red bows, and white straw hats with red ribbons around them. Despite their ages they were graceful and all knew very well the steps of the dances. Looking at Susie I saw tears in her eyes as she said, "Oh aunt Ibi how wonderful what the old generation are able to do! I wish my parents could be here or that they could have a life like this at home. Our old people at home have no respect and they are a burden for the community."

Susie was also impressed with my many activities. She even came one Tuesday night to see me in my folk dance class in Earl Bales Park and she watched us through the entire two hours. She also came on Thursday afternoon to the Baycrest Terrace where I volunteered to read my stories in Hungarian to a little group of Hungarian residents.

One day we took Susie and her children to Cullen Gardens near Whitby. This was a type of place which I knew could not be found in Hungary. In the middle of a gorgeous and beautifully kept park there was a miniature village, a replica of the village of Whitby. There was everything from the general store to the fire station. On the streets all types of houses, some with a swimming pool at the front, playgrounds with children, cars, people, little dogs on the streets and everything else to be found in a village. We even saw a house in flames and fire fighters working on the roof. There was also the miniature replica of the Canadian National Exhibition with all of the activities which it houses.

We also took them to the world's highest tower, the C.N. Tower, and it was the first time they saw and sat in a revolving restaurant at the top of the tower. They were sorry they couldn't visit another unique place, the Holocaust Education and Memorial Centre, where I also do some volunteer work in the museum. Before Susie and her children left for Hungary they promised to visit our beautiful Toronto again.

Book of Tears

I put down the little book I received from the Jewish Congress of Pécs in 1987 and covering my eyes with my hands I cried and cried.

The little eight by six inch book had a black cover and a black silk cord to keep the pages together. The title *Book of Tears* was written with gold letters in Hungarian and Hebrew. Why did I get so emotional when there are no sad stories in the book? As a matter of fact there are no stories in it at all. On every page, in a black frame, there are names. Four thousand of them! Names of the Jewish martyrs who were deported and killed from my home town, Pécs. As I read the familiar names a kaleidoscope of pictures ran through my mind.

In alphabetical order I looked up my father's name first, **Szalai Ignacz**. I see myself as a little girl in our small tinsmith shop. I liked to watch my father's skilful hands work as he made cans, buckets, cakepans and other household items from tin. The whole city knew him because his honesty, integrity and diligence made his name well-known. I recall an episode which suggests how well-known he really was. His tinsmith shop was on Iranyi Daniel Square, No. 5. The name Iranyi, Daniel commemorated a very famous man who invented matches. One day my father received a letter addressed to Mr. Iranyi, Daniel in Szalai Ignacz Square. The postman delivered the letter to my father with no problem.

When I received this book on my request from the Jewish Congress I received the following note, "The president of the Jewish Congress of Pécs remembers your father very well. He even remembers that there were three steps to enter your father's shop." I was very touched that after so many decades people still remembered my father.

Szalai Laura. I read the next name, my mother. A small woman, a little on the plump side, whose dark hair had just started to grey. She worked so hard all her life, taking care of the household, raising five daughters, and helping out in father's little shop. When she could have been taking her life easier after the last of the girls got married mother was taken away with the rest of the four thousand.

The next few names are **Stern Miksa**, his wife and four of their five children; **Tibor**, **Zoltan**, **Eva** and my best friend, **Gizi**. I remember when the older children were about fourteen and fifteen years old their mother got pregnant. She asked them if they wanted the baby or if she should have an abortion. The children wanted the baby so in a few months their little sister, Eva, was born. In 1943, during a visit to my parents with my baby son, we took an excursion with the Stern family. While we ate our lunch we talked about children among other topics. Suddenly six-year-old Eva remarked, "I know how babies are born."

"How do you know darling? Would you tell me?" I asked the little girl and then I added, "I would like to know also."

"I found out from the big book with many pictures in it from the shelf," Eva replied. Then looking around she pointed to my infant son and she said in a hushed voice, "I can't tell now because the baby would overhear it."

Turning the page I see the name **Dr. Sebok Sandor**. He was the boy who escorted me home once and who won my mother's heart when he simply accepted the watermelon she offered him.

I see my sister, Margaret's, name. She was the oldest one who had a short-lived happiness with a man but couldn't marry him because he was gentile.

My other sister's name, Ilona. She was happily married and was only 39 years old. Her son's name, George, next. George was eighteen years old when he was deported. He was still alive when the Americans liberated the camp he was in. They separated the very sick and those who had diarrhoea. The boy had the latter. During the night George sneaked out of his room and stole some food. But his starved stomach couldn't tolerate the food he ate and he died the next morning.

The next familiar name is that of **Dr. Wallenstein Zoltan**. The chief rabbi of Pécs. He was the most handsome man I ever saw. I was thirteen and very much in love with him. I still hear his deep-toned voice as he recited the prayer to a group of

young girls all in white on our batmitzvah.
Ernest Geza, I read on. Our cantor with a clear, silver-toned voice. I could listen to him for hours. I still treasure one of his records with the beautiful melody of *Kol-Nidre* which is the opening song on the highest holy day, *Jom Kippur*.

Thousands and thousands of names. Thousands and thousands of memories.

Epilogue

When in the early spring of the year 1989 I received an invitation from the Jewish Congress of Pécs for the 45th commemoration of the deportation of the four thousand Jews I had a strong urge to go. I felt that I owed it to the memory of my parents to say a prayer at the martyr's monument in the cemetery. I made a three-day hotel reservation through the Jewish Congress. My husband and I arrived in Pécs from Budapest on a Friday morning, 30 June 1989. Stepping from the train I had very mixed feelings seeing my birthplace after over forty years.

Our first step was to go to the Jewish Congress' office where they welcomed us warmly and told us about the services. It was still early in the afternoon so I took my camera and went to see our small, old family house on Alsohavi Street, number 17. I even planned to ask permission from the present owner to go in and look around the house of my childhood. With throbbing heart I finally reached the familiar street but there was no number 17. All the houses from number 9 to seventeen were in ruins.

Standing there I recalled the little house with its three windows facing the street, the two high steps which led to the heavy door, and the bell on the side which rang so many times a day because children liked to ring it just for fun. As I stood there a woman passing asked if I was looking for someone. "Yes," I replied. "I'm looking for my past." Then I asked about the houses and she told me that the city had torn them down about four years before and they hadn't cleaned up the ruins to that date.

I turned and walked over to my father's little tinsmith shop on Iranyi Daniel Square. Not much luck there either. Where the shop had once stood I found only new apartment buildings and a big patch of bare ground. In my mind's eye I saw my father's store with him inside working diligently and skilfully on household items. I slowly turned and walked towards the synagogue and the Jewish elementary school next door. The school had become a Catholic college and the synagogue was a tourist attraction during the summer. It still belonged to the Jewish Congress but it is open only on high holy days and special occasions. There is a small prayer house beside the synagogue where my husband and I went to the service Friday night. We found about twenty-five worshippers from a remaining population of 200 Jews. There is a cantor but no rabbi. A rabbi travels to the city from Budapest every second week for the Sabbath service.

Sunday morning we visited a building that had once been the ghetto on the outskirts of the city. This huge house resembled a military barracks and was home to railway employees and their families before the ghetto and now was again. This house had been vacated to form the ghetto and the Jewish population had been jammed into it. On an outside wall of the house is a plaque marking it as the Jewish ghetto of 1944.

On this Sunday the representatives of the city, the province, and the railway workers placed their wreaths and said a few words. Then the rabbi made a short speech and he and the members of the Jewish Congress also placed their wreath which was decorated with blue and white ribbons, the colours of the flag of Israel. After the ceremony I stepped into the courtyard of the house behind the gate. I looked up to the small windows wondering which room my parents, two sisters and their family might have been squeezed into before they were taken away in the cattle cars on their long and painful ride to the gaschambers. I felt completely alone as I leaned on the wall and buried my face in my palms and cried my heart out.

On the same afternoon the Memorial Service took place in the synagogue. In his speech the rabbi said, "In this beautiful synagogue which was full of worshippers before the Holocaust, only a few of us remain. Unfortunately, we can't fill the synagogue any more." As I listened I saw the synagogue many decades before, full of worshippers on Friday nights, Saturday mornings and on holy days. Returning to the present I was surprised to hear the rabbi in his mournful speech quote from a famous poem which Hungarians repeat immediately after the national anthem. The poem, titled "Appeal," was written by Mihaly Vorosmarty, an immortal name for Hungarians. However, we Hungarian Jews could no longer associate with those verses.

Be true the land of thy birth,
Son of the Magyar race;
It gave thee life, and soon its earth
Will be thy resting-place.

Although the world is very wide,
This is thy home for aye;
Come weal or woe on fortune's tide;
Here thou must live and die.
　　　(translated by W. Jaffery)

The rabbi finished with his own words, "Not only did they not let us live in our country, they even sent us somewhere else to die."

After the speech the rabbi and cantor took out a large black-covered book under a glass case in front of the Torah cabinet. The book is the enlarged copy of the *Book of Tears* which I had received from the Jewish Congress of Pécs years before. The rabbi read the opening words:

> The Book of Tears was written for future generations, to keep the names of the community's martyrs, those who were killed by fire, water, starvation, plagues and by the merciless and cruel hands of their fellow human beings during the Holocaust in the year
>
> 1940 – 1944
> *
> God must bring judgement over those evil ones who shed the blood of innocents.

After the service there were two coaches waiting to take us to the cemetery. In the cemetery we gathered around a monument which was a smaller imitation of the "Wailing Wall" in Jerusalem. The inscription on it reads:

The city of Fecs' remaining Jewish population mourns for their four thousand deported brothers and sisters.

*

Pregnant young mothers with their children under their heart, tiny babies, school-age boys and girls, teenage youngsters, God's rose garden of beautiful children, mothers and fathers, strong and weak, old and sick were dropped with tremendous suffering and humiliation into death.

In front of the monument a black flag swayed in the light wind and flowers were placed at the base of the monument by the mourners. After the *kaddish*, the prayer for the dead, the rabbi led us to a tombstone laid flat on the ground and surrounded by flowers. The inscription on the tombstone read:

RIF Soap made from the corpses of the martyrs of Auschwitz.

When I asked what *RIF* meant I was told it was an abbreviation of three German words *Reine Izraelishe Fat*. One survivor had taken a piece of that soap home and it was buried in the cemetery. I had heard this story of the soap before but I can't describe my shock and disbelief at actually seeing the tombstone with its incredible inscription.

The next morning we left my hometown which was full of sad memories. But still, I was glad that I had gone back because I made a little bit of peace with myself to attend those services. I felt I had come to a late funeral for my loved ones; a funeral which never would have been possible because millions more had been thrown into a common grave in the place called Auschwitz.

*

And now, I have finished my life-story in the beginning of a brand new year, 1990. I pray and hope that the good Lord will

give me some more years in good health so that I will be able
to see my grandchildren grow to be decent Canadian citizens
with professions of their own liking and choosing.